CLIMBER'S GUIDE TO THE
OLYMPIC MOUNTAINS

Climber's Guide

to the OLYMPIC

MOUNTAINS

OLYMPIC MOUNTAIN RESCUE

THE MOUNTAINEERS *Seattle*

Based on a previous edition published by
THE AMERICAN ALPINE CLUB

Library of Congress Catalog Card Number 70-163356

Printed in the United States of America

Published by The Mountaineers
P.O. Box 122
Seattle, Washington 98111

Frontispiece: *The South Brother from the North Brother* (Dave Haley)
Memorial: *George W. Martin* (Dave Sicks)

Upper Lena Lake and Mt. Bretherton (George W. Martin)

IN MEMORY OF

GEORGE W. MARTIN
1901–1970

WHOSE ACCOMPLISHMENTS DURING NEARLY FORTY YEARS OF
MOUNTAINEERING ARE TOO NUMEROUS TO LIST . . .

WHO ALMOST SINGLE-HANDEDLY ESTABLISHED THE OLYMPIC COLLEGE
MOUNTAINEERING AND OUTDOOR EDUCATION PROGRAM IN SPITE
OF OVERWHELMING OPPOSITION FROM THOSE WHO FELT THAT
PEOPLE SHOULD STAY OUT OF THE MOUNTAINS . . .

WHO WAS THE GUIDING FORCE AND CATALYST BEHIND ESTABLISHMENT
OF OLYMPIC MOUNTAIN RESCUE . . .

WHOM WE WILL ALWAYS BEST REMEMBER AS A FRIEND AND
CLIMBING PARTNER . . .

WHOSE UNFLAGGING DEVOTION TO MOUNTAINEERING AND CONSTANT
ENCOURAGEMENT TO OTHERS CAN ONLY BE EXPRESSED BY
HIS OWN EXHORTATION:

"TO REST IS NOT TO CONQUER"

CONTENTS

ILLUSTRATIONS

MOUNTAIN SAFETY TECHNIQUES

PHOTOGRAPHS

FOREWORD

Preparation of the *Climber's Guide to the Olympic Mountains* has been Olympic Mountain Rescue's most difficult operation. A mountain rescue unit is intimately acquainted with nighttime call-outs and the ensuing accelerated action to give assistance to some unfortunate mountain traveler. We were not aware, however, that our decision to build a guidebook would be followed by over two years of meetings, discussions, and waste baskets full of discarded manuscripts. Such mental childbearing has naturally made us quite proud of the end product.

Most of the routes listed herein have been "done" by at least one member of the Unit. Great care has been taken to transform this knowledge into accurate and understandable route descriptions. To further eliminate confusion, the route descriptions incorporate definite landmarks, known elevations, and travel times where pertinent. We only hope that this effort will enable the mountaineer, the ski tourer, or the adventuresome hiker to enjoy the Olympics as we do.

With publication of the Olympic Guide, we are almost certain that more people will find their way into this wilderness range. That the Olympics seem relatively untouched is not accidental, for true mountaineers feel a sense of responsibility to those that follow in their footsteps: a responsibility to leave the natural habitat as unspoiled as they found it. With a little effort by all, we can keep the Olympics beautiful for everyone. "Leave nothing but footprints, take nothing but memories."

We sincerely hope that the reader's experience in this range is an enjoyable one, unmarred by either incident or injury. Happy climbing!

HAROLD L. PINSCH
Chairman, Olympic Mountain Rescue

January, 1971

ACKNOWLEDGMENTS

Since this book is a third generation guide to climbers in the Olympic Mountains, special acknowledgment is given to the preceding efforts from which this guidebook grew. In this respect, Fred Beckey leads all others, for it was his vision and almost single-handed effort that created the original *Climber's Guide to the Cascades and Olympics*. Next, George Sainsbury and his committee of The American Alpine Club should be remembered for their fine work leading to the 1961 edition of the same publication. Finally, appreciation is expressed to The American Alpine Club for their cooperation and permission for us to use their previously copyrighted manuscript.

Development of this volume was a team effort from beginning to end and I am extremely grateful for the unwavering dedication of each "member" throughout what became a long and difficult task. Equally important was the continuing support of Olympic Mountain Rescue and particularly that of Chairman Harold Pinsch, for without their confidence this book could not have been written. Next, my personal thanks to George Sainsbury for his exceptional contributions, a gamut of tasks too numerous to describe. George's knowledge of guidebooks was freely given and without his counsel my own task would have been much more difficult.

Every effort has been expended to acknowledge each individual who contributed to this volume. If anyone has been missed, please accept my sincere apologies. The contributors are as follows:

Those responsible for research and preparation of one or more manuscript sections were Arnold Bloomer, Roy Etten, Jack Hughes, Glenn Kelsey, Harold Pinsch, George Sainsbury and Keith Spencer.

We were fortunate to have the help of two fine artists, and the art work speaks for itself. Dee Molenaar prepared the peak sketches; Kent Heathershaw developed the sketch maps and provided other support. The literary editing was professionally accomplished by Edward M. Matthews. Manuscript typing, a long and demanding task, was capably handled by Joyce Magnusson. Special contributions included Richard Culp, George W. Martin and Dave Sicks for photography support; Paul Williams for legal counsel; Dr. Robert Yekel for medical counsel.

Others who contributed material or were otherwise helpful in various ways include Don N. Anderson, Roger Beckett, Fred Beckey, Bert Brown, Tom Chandler, Jack Christiansen, Loraine Debuque, Eiichi Fukushima, John Gray, Curt Howard, Neal Jacques, Ruth Jewell, Ron Kaiser, Oiva Knute, Ed LaChapelle, Joe Munson, Fred Natter, Jack Newman, Sandy Newman, Richard Olson Jr., Richard Pargeter, Mary Jane Sainsbury, Roy Sederberg, Gordon Sinrud, Jan Spencer, Roland Tabor, Robert Yeats, Fritz Wiessner, Ben West, Marilyn West, and Robert Wood.

This list of credits would not be complete without acknowledging the role of The Mountaineers who, as publisher, accomplished the final critical step toward making this book available to the climbing public. In this regard, Harvey Manning, Tom Miller, John Pollock, Howard Stansbury and the rest of the Literary Fund Committee should be specifically thanked.

Last but not least, to our wives a standing ovation. During the entire two years they stood behind us offering hospitality, support and, above all, patience.

F. KEITH SPENCER
Chairman, Olympic Guidebook Committee

CLIMBER'S GUIDE TO THE OLYMPIC MOUNTAINS

INTRODUCTION

The Olympic Mountains occupy the center of the Olympic Peninsula, which is bounded on the south by the lowlands of the Chehalis valley, on the east by Hood Canal, on the north by the Strait of Juan de Fuca, and on the west by the Pacific Ocean. Although neither high nor extensive, they present an imposing barrier to the winds which sweep in from the sea. Captain John Meares, the English navigator who sighted the major uplift from shipboard in 1788, is supposed to have said, "If that be not the home where dwell the gods, it is certainly beautiful enough to be, and I therefore will call it Mt. Olympus." He was unaware that the Spanish navigator Juan Perez had previously named the peaks "Sierra Nevada de Santa Rosalia" in 1774. Meares' name was used by Captain George Vancouver, and as Spanish influence waned it was generally adopted by the British and extended to the whole peninsula. The mountains, however, continued to be called the "Coast Range" until 1849, when Hall J. Kelley and J. Quinn Thornton made their well-publicized attempt to change the name of the Cascades to "President's Range" and also proposed that Mt. Olympus be designated "Mt. Van Buren." The effort failed, and in 1864 the Seattle *Weekly Gazette* was successful in getting the name "Olympic Mountains" officially adopted. Thus the colorful Duwamish Indian name for the range, "Sun-a-do," and the Clallam Indian name, which translated to "Thunderbird," were forgotten among the conflicting proposals of the white man.

The Olympics stand alone, isolated from other mountains, and rise from bases just barely above sea level to heights of nearly

3

8000 feet. These mountains are not a "range" in the usual sense; rather, they comprise a compact cluster of steep peaks surrounded by a belt of densely timbered foothills. The drainage system is radial, with river valleys penetrating deeply into the mountain mass from all sides. The sources of most of the rivers are in the snowfields and glaciers of the higher peaks near the center of the uplift, and the mountains are deeply dissected by wild, rugged canyons carved by gushing torrents and carpeted by green jungles of slide alder, vine maple, and devil's club. Some valleys provide an extremely hostile environment for travel, notorious for box canyons and frequent cliffy waterfalls. When the downward plunge of the rushing streams eases, perhaps 1000 feet above sea level, the valleys become broader and frequently provide easier travel.

West Peak of the Anderson Massif is the hydrographic apex of the Olympic Peninsula, with its waters flowing into Hood Canal, the Strait of Juan de Fuca, and the Pacific Ocean. The major rivers draining the mountains westward to the Pacific are the Soleduck, Bogachiel, Hoh, Queets, and Quinault. The Skokomish, Hamma Hamma, Duckabush, Dosewallips, and Quilcene Rivers flow eastward into Hood Canal. The Strait of Juan de Fuca to the north receives the waters of the Elwha River, and the Dungeness River with its large tributaries, Grand Creek, Cameron Creek, and Gray Wolf River. The Humptulips, Wynoochee, and Satsop Rivers drain southward into the Chehalis valley and Grays Harbor.

Lying across the prevailing westerly winds, the seaward slopes of these mountains are deluged by the heaviest precipitation in the forty-eight conterminous states. The average rainfall at Hoh Ranger Station is 142 inches per year, and Mt. Olympus receives the equivalent of more than 220 inches annually. As a result, the western lowlands support a climax forest of spruce and hemlock. Sitka spruce, mostly below 1000 feet in elevation, averages 220 feet in height, and may reach 300 feet. Western hemlock is most common from 1500 feet to 3000 feet, and the largest known specimen is on the East Fork of the Quinault River near Enchanted Valley. Though Douglas-fir is less common in the

Olympics than in the Cascades, occasional groves occur. The world's largest recorded Douglas-fir is located just off the Kloochman Peak trail, 3 miles up the Queets River from road end. Western redcedar is still more infrequent, though the largest known specimen, with a diameter of 21'4", is located near Kalaloch. The western Olympics also contain record specimens of Pacific silver fir and Sub-alpine fir.

Another result of the extreme rainfall is the extensive permanent snowfields and glaciers above 5000 feet. There are at least seventy of these, even though the highest summit in the range is less than 8000 feet in elevation. The glaciers are centered on the Mt. Olympus Massif, in the northern Bailey Range, and on Mt. Anderson, with a scattering of smaller permanent glaciers and snowfields on other peaks. Mt. Olympus ranks third in the amount of glaciation on a single peak in the forty-eight contiguous states, with the Hoh Glacier being the longest in the Olympics. Crevasses with a depth of more than 150 feet and a width of more than 30 feet are not uncommon in this area.

Most of the major peaks in the Olympic Mountains are not difficult to climb by the standard established routes. However, widely separated parts of the range provide challenging rock climbing—especially Sawtooth Ridge above Flapjack Lakes, The Needles in the Royal Basin area, and the Mt. Constance Massif. Snow and ice climbers find the greatest attraction to be the glaciers of Mt. Olympus, but many peaks provide excellent snow climbing early in the season. Mt. Constance and Inner Constance give the climber a good variety of mixed climbing, some of the routes being quite difficult. The outstanding appeal and charm of the Olympics, however, is in the abundant availability of relatively untouched wilderness, which together with the unpredictable weather and variety of terrain provides great challenges in wilderness navigation.

Though the interior is liberally crossed with access trails, these usually follow major river valleys. Even the better-known high routes, such as the Bailey Range traverse through fabled Cream Lake Basin, or the Glacier Meadows-Elwha Basin traverse through Blizzard Pass and Queets Basin, are visited only a few times a year. Such relatively unknown areas as the upper Goldie or Queets drainages, the high alpine country between Mt. Christie, Mt. Anderson, and the Enchanted Valley, or the inaccessable peaks north and east of Mt. Carrie, may see only one or two parties in a decade.

History of Exploration and Mountaineering

The general history of the taming and settlement of the periphery of the peninsula and the establishment of the national park is thoroughly recorded in a number of popular books, so it will not be covered here. The mountains themselves, however, were almost totally unexplored until shortly before the turn of the century. Both the formal and informal penetration of the range proceeded more or less simultaneously, the former well organized, documented, and publicized, and the latter generally unknown except to the participants and their immediate friends.

The "mountain men" were mostly local settlers in the Port Angeles area, or homesteaders who staked their homesites up the verdant valleys that penetrate the north and west sides of the range. These men roamed the range partly to hunt and fish, partly because they loved the high country in the same sense as a modern climber. One of the better known "mountain men," Billy Everett, is reported to have reached Cream Lake Basin as early as 1885. A party from the Port Townsend area penetrated all the way to Queets Basin via Dodwell-Rixon Pass in 1894. The Humes brothers, Will and Grant, roamed widely throughout the Elwha drainage and the adjacent high country. No doubt these men and others like them climbed many of the less difficult peaks but left no record. Little is known of the exploits of most of the "mountain men," so their accomplishments as well as their names will probably remain unrecorded.

Lt. Joseph P. O'Neil, earliest of the leaders of organized exploration, became interested in the early 1880s, after taking part in a discussion with other Army officers concerning the lack of knowledge of the interior. He impulsively volunteered to lead the exploration, and was soon dispatched from Fort Vancouver to Port Townsend with five enlisted men and three civilian engineers to undertake the task. In the summer of 1885, the first of the O'Neil parties pushed up the Elwha and Hayes Rivers to the vicinity of Hayden Pass. O'Neil may have climbed Mt. Claywood and Mt. Fromme—certainly he named the former for Clay Wood, the Assistant Adjutant General who signed his orders. He was summarily recalled in midsummer and sent east for training, but his desire to complete the exploration of the Olympics remained undimmed.

In 1888 Eugene Semple, the last Territorial Governor of Washington, devoted a major portion of his report to the U.S. Department of the Interior to the riddle of the Olympics. Elisha P. Ferry, first elected Governor of the State of Washington, was so impressed with his predecessor's report that he encouraged the Seattle *Press* to organize an expedition. Throughout the winter of 1889–1890, the Press Expedition under the leadership of James H. Christie fought against unbelievable odds up the Elwha and Goldie Rivers, finally crossing Low Divide to the North Fork of the Quinault River and arriving at Lake Quinault in June. Captain Charles A. Barnes, the expedition cartographer, produced the first reasonably accurate map of the interior, and the whole epic was published in a special 24-page edition of the *Press* on July 16, 1890.

One of the reasons for haste on the part of the Press party was the fear of being "scooped." They almost were, for in October, 1889, S. C. Gilman and his father, C. S. Gilman, the Lieutenant Governor of Minnesota, ascended the Quinault River by canoe, then continued overland to Anderson Pass before returning the way they had come in late November. This trip was reported only briefly in the media, and was not generally known until *National Geographic* published the account in April, 1896.

William G. Steel of Portland, who later founded the Mazamas, had organized the Oregon Alpine Club in 1887, and since that time had been trying to interest the U.S. Army in resuming Lt. O'Neil's work. When O'Neil was again posted to Fort Vancouver early in 1890, he found his superiors cooperative, and with

Steel's help he quickly assembled a party primarily composed of enlisted men and members of the Oregon Alpine Club. He was able to obtain an advance copy of the Press Expedition report, and set off across the range from the Skokomish River approach. The travel was incredibly difficult, since trails had to be built for pack animals. But with the help of the Hoquiam Board of Trade which built 30 miles of trail to meet him from the coastal approach, he eventually crossed First Divide, ascended the Duckabush River to O'Neil Pass, and descended the Enchanted Valley to Lake Quinault.

The O'Neil Expedition completed a prodigious amount of work, with side parties exploring and mapping the drainages of the Duckabush, Hamma Hamma, North and South Forks of the Skokomish, Humptulips, Wynoochee, Satsop, North and East Forks of the Quinault, and Queets Rivers. The expedition is best remembered, however, for the first attempted ascent of Mt. Olympus. The earlier reported ascent in 1854 by five white men and four Makah Indians is now generally discounted by scholars.

Lt. O'Neil dispatched N. E. Linsley and B. J. Bretherton of the Oregon Alpine Club, Sgt. F. W. Yates, and four privates, to climb Mt. Olympus. They followed the North Fork of the Quinault River to Low Divide, occasionally finding traces of the preceding Press party. Here they continued north and west to Queets Basin, where Private Fisher became separated from the main party and eventually found his way out the Queets canyon to the Pacific, no mean accomplishment. The remainder of the party continued around the Humes Glacier to the vicinity of Blizzard Pass, where they describe the Hoh Glacier with great accuracy. But instead of ascending the Hoh, they then proceeded west onto either the Jeffers or Hubert Glacier and made the final climb from the south on September 22, 1890. Linsley, Bretherton, and Private Danton were in the summit party, and they left a copper box near the top containing the record of the climb, a deck of cards, two army buttons, and various other mementos as a permanent record of the first ascent. The copper box has never been located, and just which peak was ascended by the O'Neil Expedition remains a mystery to this day.

During the summer of 1890 Judge James W. Wickersham of Tacoma, who later made the first attempt on Mt. McKinley in 1903, led a party up the Skokomish with the intent of crossing the range and descending the valley of the Quinault. After great hardship, one member of the party became ill from poison ivy, and the group came out the Dosewallips valley. After the many efforts of 1890 the public considered the mountains largely explored, and they attracted little attention for the next 15 years, with few visitors other than the "mountain men" traveling beyond the foothills.

When President Grover Cleveland created the Olympic Forest Reserve of 2,168,320 acres by proclamation in 1897, the Department of the Interior ordered a survey. The U.S. Geological Survey employed Theodore Rixon and Arthur Dodwell to complete this work, and for 3 years, from 1898 to 1900, these men and their four assistants toiled tirelessly, working in the high country in the summer and the foothills in the winter, and climbing many of the peaks for pleasure as much as duty. In all, they surveyed 97 townships or partial townships, 3483 square miles. Only 16 of these square miles had been logged. The total was staggering—61 billion board feet of timber in the reserve alone. The records of their ascents are lost forever, but their exploration was so thorough and meticulous that it can be assumed they climbed all of the peaks which were not either technically difficult or far removed from timber or alpine meadows. We know they climbed Mt. Carrie, Mt. Queets, and Mt. Noyes, from interviews with Rixon late in his life.

In August, 1899, the Dodwell-Rixon team was encamped near Blizzard Pass high on the divide between the Hoh and Humes Glaciers. After conjecture that the summit of Olympus was virgin, Jack McGlone, one of the packers, set off alone at dusk for the ascent. Reaching the top, he recorded his account on a clipping from a Shelton newspaper and left it in a tin box. McGlone's clipping was recovered in 1907 on the 7780-foot East Peak when the second ascent was made by a party from The Mountaineers. Dodwell and Rixon accepted McGlone's notes for their report, and thus missed a chance for the highest

summit, for the entire party had planned to climb it the following day.

1907 was the great year for Mt. Olympus. The Mountaineers,
newly formed in Seattle, selected this still-unclimbed summit as
their first major objective, and carefully planned the expedition
to conquer it. An advance scouting party from the club climbed
Queets and Noyes in May, and trail-building crews prepared the
way up the Elwha valley throughout June and July. But in mid-
July, a fortnight before the scheduled arrival of The Mountaineers, a team of three representing the American Geographical
Society arrived in Port Angeles from New York with the
avowed intent of climbing Mt. Olympus. Little is known of Wal-
ter G. Clarke, but Professor Hershell C. Parker and Belmore H.
Browne were among the foremost American climbers of the day.
Browne was rapidly gaining fame as a mountain artist; Parker
had been one of the founders of the fledgling American Alpine
Club. Both were members of the prestigious Explorers Club and
had accompanied Dr. Frederick A. Cook in his attempt on Mt.
McKinley in the preceding year. With two local packers they ascended the Elwha Snow Finger, crossed Dodwell-Rixon Pass,
which they named for the survey team, and placed their last
camp near the foot of the Humes Glacier, which they christened
for one of their packers. They gained the summit of the Middle
Peak on July 17th, and thinking it to be the highest in the broken clouds, returned triumphantly to civilization and announced
that Olympus had been climbed.

The newspaper publicity was extensive, and The Mountaineers
were incensed, for the eastern party had hired their packers,
used their approach trail, and "stolen" their peak. Parker and
Browne were especially vulnerable to criticism, for they had ac-
cused Dr. Cook, a national hero, of falsifying his claim to the
first ascent of Mt. McKinley, and they had not yet been able to
prove their contention. Some local climbers claimed that but for
the skill of Will Humes the party would not have been able to
make the climb, an absurdity when one considers that in 1912
Parker and Browne came within 300 feet of the summit of Mt.
McKinley. On the other hand, at least one eastern writer was

still crediting them with the first ascent of Mt. Olympus as recently as 1946.

Against this emotionally-charged background The Mountaineers set forth with heavy heart, for it was too late for them to change their outing to another area. After climbing a number of lesser peaks, they ascended the East Peak on August 12th and found the record of Jack McGlone's lone climb. The following day a party of eleven led by L. A. Nelson climbed the Middle Peak and located the cairn left by Parker, Browne, and Clarke, then went on to the higher West Peak, and, congratulating themselves on their unbelievable good fortune, claimed the greatest prize of all.

The hard-rock miners arrived in the Olympics in the early 1900s, and by 1906 the first claims had been staked. The range is remarkably free of valuable minerals in commercial quantities, but small deposits of manganese were discovered at various points along the valleys of the eastern front range, and most of these deposits were accompanied by copper as a secondary mineral. The American Manganese Corporation established its mine at Tubal Cain in the Dungeness valley in 1908, and worked it and the satellite mine at Tull City at intermittent intervals through 1941. Other small deposits were located in the drainages of the Hamma Hamma, the Duckabush, and the Dosewallips, and some mining was carried out near Little Hump and well below timberline on the southeast shoulder of Mt. Constance. Several hundred men were employed during the peak of the activity in the Dungeness drainage, and they probably roamed extensively across the barren ridges near Mt. Townsend, Tyler Peak, Baldy, and the Buckhorn-Iron area, but no record of climbs has survived.

Following the ascent of Mt. Olympus many parties climbed extensively in the range, though some of the greatest summits remained unclimbed for decades. The Klahane Club was formed in Port Angeles in 1919, and The Olympians were founded in 1921 in Grays Harbor. The Bremerton Branch of The Mountaineers was started in 1920, and though short-lived it contributed to the establishment of the climbing tradition in Kitsap County which eventually spawned the Bremerton Alpine Club and later the Olympic College climbing program. The Mountaineers and their branches in Tacoma and Everett continued to visit the range regularly, making the first ascent of Mt. Anderson in 1920. After at least five previous attempts, Mt. Constance, the greatest remaining prize, was climbed in 1922 when A. E. "Bremerton" Smith and Robert Schellin, members of The Mountaineers, solved the approach puzzle and reached the top by a long and now seldom-used route. The Mazamas of Portland first scheduled an Olympic summer outing in 1928 and have been frequent visitors since that time.

The Boy Scouts have had a long and intimate association with the range, the earliest example of which is the first ascent of Mt. Tom by Edmond S. Meany and a Scout group in 1914. In the following years the Seattle Council established its main camp on Hood Canal, the Tumwater Council at Lower Lena Lake, and the Twin Harbors Council on Lake Quinault. The second ascent of Mt. Constance was completed by a Boy Scout party in 1923, and over a period of several decades these groups ranged widely throughout the mountains, accounting for place names such as "Lake of the Angels," "Del Monte Ridge," and "Scout Lake," and climbing a majority of the summits which did not require ropes and many of a more difficult nature. With the changes in national Scout policy in the late 40s, provisional unit camping was eliminated, and Scout use of the remote high country decreased markedly.

Theodore Roosevelt created the Mt. Olympus National Monument by proclamation in 1909, but conservationists recognized that this did not provide adequate protection, for national monuments could be reduced in size at presidential whim. Three such reductions were made between 1912 and 1929, leaving the remaining monument barely half its original size. In 1933 national monuments were transferred from the jurisdiction of the U.S. Forest Service to the National Park Service, and during this decade pressure to create a national park mounted. The Forest Service created an adjacent primitive area in 1936, in an

Mt. Olympus from the High Divide (Dave Sicks)

effort to allay the drive for park status, but this proved unsuc-
cessful, and congress created Olympic National Park in 1938.
While the park is quite large, almost 897,000 acres at present,
much of it is in the western lowlands and the coastal strip, and
many of the most prominent peaks are on the eastern border or
in Olympic National Forest. The slopes of these peaks remain
unprotected from the ravages of logging clear cuts.

Areas providing challenging rock climbing in the range are limited, and interest developed relatively late. A group from the
Bremerton Alpine Club became involved in the mid-30s, and
with a break for the Second World War, they and their succes-
sors climbed all but a few of the pinnacles on the Sawtooth
Ridge. First ascents were still being made in this area as recently
as 1960. The other main rock-climbing area in the Olympics,
The Needles, first attracted the attention of Bremerton climbers
in 1940, and the last major first ascent, The Arrowhead, was not
completed until 1962.

One of the most unusual aspects of the climbing history of the
Olympic Mountains is that so many of the highest and most
challenging summits remained virgin for so long. Despite the
tremendous post-war boom in tourism and great climbing activity on scores of peaks, most climbers seem to have clung to the
familiar mountains and routes. With only 35 peaks in the range
exceeding 7000 feet in elevation, 21 of these were still unclimbed in 1940, 13 remained in 1950, and 6 had not yet been
climbed in 1960.

Today the exploration is virtually completed and all the major
summits have been climbed. The wilderness remains as challenging as ever, though, and much of it is yet untrodden.

Geological Considerations

From the climber's viewpoint, there are three main geologic factors contributing to the most interesting peaks: the relative
hardness of the rock, the recency of sculpture by glaciation, and
the overall height of the mountain. If the rock is not more resis-
tant to erosion than surrounding rock, and the time since glacia-

tion is great or the height insignificant, the terrain has little challenge. These three factors are not independent of each other, and on any one climb other characteristics of the rock, such as the nature of the jointing, may be important.

Some of the best climbing in the Olympic Mountains is on hard basalt lavas which form partial rings around a core of sedimentary and metamorphic rocks. The lavas erupted on the ocean bottom in horizontal layers about 60 million years ago (Lower Tertiary Era) and became interlayered with sand and mud. The outermost basalt layer later bulged up like the skin of a giant blister and has been broken and breached by erosion. It now forms the most extensive and continuous ring, and offers some of the most challenging climbing. Peaks in this ring such as Constance, The Brothers, Pershing, and Lincoln stand high and steep above the more rounded ridges of sedimentary rock. The importance of relative hardness is shown by these mountains, for they have not been heavily glaciated recently except near their summits, and they are not in the highest part of the range.

An inner ring of basalts offers high-angle climbing of varying soundness in The Needles and Sawtooth Ridge. Even where the basalt is only present as relatively thin slivers it makes imposing pinnacles or faces, such as Piro's Spire, some unclimbed fangs on Cameron Creek, and Steeple Rock. Very thin slivers of basaltic rock deeper in the core of the range hold up bold faces or ridges on Mt. Fromme and Mt. Claywood and on the north ridge of Mt. Ferry.

All three factors have operated to make challenging climbs of the hard sandstone peaks of Mt. Olympus and its flanking retinue of smaller summits. Summits of phyllite or slate, on the other hand, offer very little exciting work even in the Mt. Olympus area, though they may present some imposing faces smoothed by glaciers, such as the east side of Mt. Dana or Dodger Point.

Although these factors govern the major pattern of the mountains, the details of the climb are commonly determined by the nature of the jointing. Joints are cracks formed as internal pressures release when the rocks become exposed to the earth's surface by erosion. Closely-spaced joints cause the peaks to crumble into relatively easy heaps of rubble. Widely-spaced joints leave flawless monoliths and pinnacles on the ridge tops. The basalts of Sawtooth Ridge and The Needles have widely-spaced joints. Meany, Queets, and Anderson are sandstone peaks with imposing summit blocks.

Weather

The Olympics lie in the storm belt of the Pacific, and are notorious for their highly changeable weather. Even on the leeward side of the range, precipitation is heavy and weather patterns shift with alarming rapidity. Since most of the more rewarding climbs in the range require a minimum of two to three days, it is always advisable to prepare for summer storms. Temperature variations can be as much as 70° in a 24-hour period in the high interior, and it is not uncommon to experience clear skies and debilitating heat followed by clouds, rain, and driving sleet, in the course of a single summer afternoon. The so-called "rain shadow" of the Olympics is an exception to this pattern, and weather in this sheltered area which is protected by the high mountains to the west and south is much more stable and salubrious. This belt comprises the lower drainages of the Gray Wolf, Cameron, Grand, Dungeness, and Quilcene Rivers, as well as all of the rock-climbing areas in The Needles.

Changes in weather patterns in the interior of the range are frequently of relatively long duration. It is not uncommon to have several days or weeks of splendid weather followed by an extended period of more than a week of heavy summer rain and chilling temperatures. Storms usually blow in from the southwest or west, though there are occasional exceptions. Typical signs of weather change consist of an advancing and thickening line of cirrus or cirro-stratus clouds, often followed within 24 hours by a frontal system. Thunderstorms seldom occur in these mountains, though lightning, if it occurs, is as great a hazard here as elsewhere.

Access

The Olympic Peninsula is easily reached from Puget Sound cities by car, using cross-Sound ferries and the Olympic Highway (U.S. 101) which surrounds the mountains. The Aberdeen-Hoquiam area is served by Hughes Air West with regularly scheduled flights, and bus service is available on the highway. Spur roads from the Olympic Highway follow various river valleys into the interior. The Hurricane Ridge road, the Olympic Hot Springs road, the Sol Duc Hot Springs road, and the Hoh River road are paved. Other roads are gravel, and are generally in fair condition. All roads end at low elevations except the Deer Park and Hurricane Ridge roads. Detailed information on access to specific climbing areas is included in the introduction to each climbing section.

Maps

One of the advantages enjoyed by climbers in this range is complete coverage by relatively high-quality USGS topographic quadrangles of reasonably recent vintage. The endpaper at the back of this book indicates the location and interrelation of topographic quadrangles. The USGS also publishes a 30′ topographic map of Olympic National Park in both regular and shaded-relief editions. Further updating of some key maps is now underway, and more recent editions should be available in a few years. The date of issue of USGS maps in the mountainous areas of the peninsula is as follows:

7½′ Quadrangles		*15′ Quadrangles*	
Mt. Muller	1950	Mt. Tom	1956
Lake Crescent	1950	Mt. Olympus	1956
Lake Sutherland	1950	Mt. Angeles	1944
Elwha	1950	Tyler Peak	1946
Port Angeles	1961	Kloochman Rock	1956
Slide Peak	1950	Mt. Christie	1947
Bogachiel Peak	1950	Mt. Steel	1947
Mt. Carrie	1950	The Brothers	1947
Hurricane Hill	1950	Quinault Lake	1955
		Grisdale	1955
		Mt. Tebo	1953

Topographic quadrangles are available by mail from the Distribution Section, Geological Survey, Federal Center, Denver, Colorado 80225. They may also be purchased over the counter from the following outlets in northwestern Washington:

> Alpine Hut, 2650 University Village, Seattle
> Black and King, 2944 Colby Avenue, Everett
> Captains, two locations in Seattle
> Griggs, 120 East Holly Street, Bellingham
> Metzger Maps, stores in Seattle and Tacoma
> Montesano Hardware, 210 S. Main Street, Montesano
> Recreational Equipment, Inc., two locations in Seattle

The Olympics in Relief, a shaded relief map not providing contour lines, is published by George Martin and Richard Pargeter and is available at most of the above outlets and various other retail stores in the area.

Planimetric Forest Service maps are available through Olympic National Forest headquarters in Olympia, or at any of the Forest Service ranger stations. In addition to the map of the total forest, ranger district sheets can be obtained in the following combinations: Shelton-Quinault, Quilcene-Hoodsport, and Soleduck.

References

Trail Country - Olympic National Park, by Robert L. Wood, The Mountaineers, Seattle, 1968. 298 pages.

Exploring the Olympic Peninsula, by Ruth Kirk, University of Washington Press. Seattle, revised edition 1967. 118 pages.

Roads and Trails of Olympic National Park, by Frederick Leissler, University of Washington Press, Seattle, second revised edition 1971. 114 pages.

Wilderness Trails of Olympic National Park, by Robert L. Wood, The Mountaineers, Seattle, 1970. 219 pages.

Olympic National Park - Washington, by Gunnar O. Fagerlund, Government Printing Office, Washington D.C., revised edition 1965. 60 pages.

Across the Olympic Mountains - The Press Expedition 1889–90, by Robert L. Wood, The Mountaineers and the University of Washington Press, Seattle, 1967. 220 pages.

100 Hikes in Western Washington, by Louise B. Marshall, The Mountaineers, Seattle, 1966. 224 pages.

Trips and Trails 1, by E. M. Sterling, The Mountaineers, Seattle, 1967. 211 pages.

The Olympic Rain Forest, by Ruth Kirk, University of Washington Press, Seattle, 1966. 96 pages.

101 Wildflowers of Olympic National Park, by Grant and Wenonah Sharpe, University of Washington Press, Seattle, 1954. 40 pages.

Roosevelt Elk of Olympic National Park, by Coleman C. Newman, Olympic Natural History Association, Port Angeles, 1958. 22 pages.

Common Birds of Olympic National Park, by Eugene J. Wilhelm, Jr., Olympic Natural History Association, Port Angeles, 1961. 54 pages.

Geology of Olympic National Park, by Wilbert R. Danner, University of Washington Press, Seattle, 1955. 68 pages.

Lakes of Washington - Volume 1, Western Washington, by E. E. Walcott, Washington State Division of Water Resources, Olympia, revised edition 1966. 620 pages.

The Untamed Olympics, by Ruby El Hult, Binfords and Mort, Portland, 1954. 267 pages.

102 Hikes in the Alpine Lakes, South Cascades, and Olympics, by Ira Spring and Harvey Manning, The Mountaineers, Seattle, 1971. 240 pages.

Climbing Regulations

Olympic National Park has no climbing regulations, but recommends registering for climbs. The Park does enforce some rules pertaining to backcountry usage, primarily regarding fire control, domestic animals, sanitation, and protection of wildlife and the wilderness. Since these regulations change from time to time, it is recommended that the climber obtain a current copy of *Backcountry Guide,* the free pamphlet provided by the Park Service for wilderness users in the Olympics.

Rating System

The Modified NCCS, a marriage of the National Climbing Classification System and the Sierra Decimal System, was selected for use in this guidebook because it was felt that it most nearly satisfied the rating problems found in the Olympics, such as an abundance of snow, long arduous approaches, the relative difficulty in route finding, and the heavy forest growth often extending into the technical portions of the route. It is the system projected for use in the forthcoming guides to the Cascade Range in Washington, and it is the system best understood by most currently active climbers in the Pacific Northwest.

Overall Difficulty. The overall difficulty of the route is represented by a Roman numeral from I through VI, with the difficulty increasing in ascending order. This rating, known as the "Grade," takes many factors into account—the length of the route in terms of both time and distance; the average difficulty of all the individual pitches; the ease of escape or retreat, if required; the extent of the weather problem, either in estimating it or in the effect of rain or snow on the route; the various objective dangers, such as avalanche or rockfall; the routefinding difficulty; and, somewhat more vaguely, the challenge or degree of commitment required by the route.

Since many factors are used to establish the overall difficulty rating, one should not expect, for example, to be able to climb all Grade III climbs just because he has been successful on one Grade III route. An experienced climber might apply the same

Grade to two climbs, even though one involved a 5.8 pitch, while the second had no pitches exceeding 5.4 in classification.

Individual Pitch Free Climbing Difficulty. Never applied to an entire climb, this rating, known as the "Class," indicates the severity of the most difficult free pitch of the route, and is signified by Arabic numbers applied in ascending order of difficulty. These numbers are loosely defined as follows:

> 1—Walking
> 2—Scrambling, some use of the hands required
> 3—Advisable to rope up, occasional belaying
> 4—Continuous belaying required for safety
> 5—Artificial means required for safety

Class 5 is further subdivided into tenths to more accurately identify the difficulty of technical climbing. A comparison of the Grade of overall difficulty with the Class of the most difficult pitch will give an experienced climber a fairly accurate indication of what can be expected.

Individual Pitch Aid Climbing Difficulty. The classification of the most difficult direct aid pitch is represented by the letter "A" (for aid) followed by an Arabic number from 1 to 5. A1 and A2 climbs can usually be done using standard iron, while specialized equipment or techniques such as short tie-off loops, knife-blade pitons, bongs, etc., will normally be required for A3, A4, or A5 climbs. Since few routes in the Olympics require direct aid, this part of the rating is usually absent.

Applying the System to the Olympic Range. Many Olympic climbs are started only after miles of approach by trail; this distance is not included as part of the rating. The classification of a route starts where the party leaves the trail, or, in a few instances, the road, if that is where the climb begins.

The Olympics are not especially well-suited to the technical specialist, and most routes included in the guide provide an overall mountaineering experience. Therefore the overall difficulty Grade as applied in this guide places increased emphasis on routefinding, wilderness travel, brush beating (some of it vertical), length of the route, friability of the rock, and objective danger, and slightly less emphasis on pure technical difficulty. This can be contrasted with the Teton Range, more suited to the technician, where the guidebook has given primary emphasis to technical climbing and less emphasis to the relatively simple and straightforward approaches.

These ratings apply to good summertime conditions. Any climb obviously increases in difficulty as conditions deteriorate. Assignment of a rating to each route was made only after considerable discussion, and was done as objectively as possible. Since ratings are, by their nature, subjective, it is expected that all climbers will not agree with the rating assigned to every route. Novices will be inclined to feel that some routes are underrated, while experts may take the opposite position.

Charts. The following charts are provided for the convenience of the climber who is not familiar with the Olympic Range or the Modified NCCS. The Pitch Classification Comparison Chart is a conversion table which makes it possible to translate "Class" ratings into the various other systems now in use. The charts of "Standard" climbs for "Grade" and "Class" for the Cascades and Olympics will give the climber a reasonably accurate understanding of the relationship of his own experience to a specific "Grade" or "Class."

PITCH CLASSIFICATION COMPARISON CHART

Modified NCCS (Used in this Guidebook)	NCCS	Sierra Decimal System	UIAA [1]	Welzenbach System (Used in 1961 Edition of the Cascade and Olympic Guide)
1	F1	1	I	1
2		2		2
3	F2	3	!I	3
4	F3	4	III −	4
5.0		5.0	III	
5.1	F4	5.1	III +	
5.2		5.2	IV −	
5.3	F5	5.3	IV	
5.4		5.4	IV +	5
5.5	F6	5.5	V −	
5.6		5.6	V	
5.7	F7	5.7	V +	
5.8	F8	5.8	VI −	
5.9	F9	5.9	VI	
5.10	F10	5.10	VI +	
A1	A1	6.0 6.1 6.2 6.3	A1	
A2	A2	6.4 6.5	A2	6
A3	A3	6.6 6.7	A3	
A4	A4	6.8	A4	
A5	A5	6.9	A5	

[1] Union Internationale des Associations d'Alpinisme. This system has been adopted by the European Federation and presumably will become standard throughout Europe. This system has gained support of some well-known American climbers and may eventually be accepted in the United States. The listed ratings are supplemented by descriptive terms and symbols. For details, see the 1969 *American Alpine Journal*, pp. 365–370.

STANDARD CLIMBS—OVERALL ROUTE DIFFICULTY, OR "GRADE"

	OLYMPICS	CASCADES
I	Mt. Buckhorn (low in grade)	Pinnacle Peak (low in grade)
	Mt. Angeles, Route 1	Silver Peak
	Mt. Carrie (from Heart Lake)	Sahale Peak
	Mt. Washington, Route 1	Kaleetan Peak
	Mt. Anderson, Route 1	Whitehorse Mtn., easiest route
	The Brothers, Route 1 (high in grade)	The Tooth, South Face Routes (high in grade)
	Mt. Cruiser, Route 1 (high in grade)	
II	Mt. Cruiser, Route 4 (low in grade)	Mt. Baker, Coleman Glacier Route
	Mt. Johnson, Route 1 (low in grade)	Forbidden Peak, easiest route
	Mt. Constance, Route 1	Mt. Rainier, Emmons, Ingraham, and Gibraltar Routes
	Mt. Olympus, Route 1	
	The Brothers, North Peak, Route 2	Mt. Stuart, West Ridge
	Chimney Peak, Route 2	Mt. Garfield, easiest route
	West Peak (Anderson Massif), Route 1	Bear's Breast, easiest route
III	Mt. Constance, Routes 2 & 5	North Peak of Mt. Index, easiest route
	Mt. Constance, Route 3 (high in the grade)	Mt. Baker, North Ridge
		Mt. Stuart, North Ridge
		Nooksack Tower
IV	None identified at this time	Mt. Rainier, Ptarmigan Ridge
		Mt. Stuart, East Face & Northeast Face Routes
		Mt. Shuksan, Northeast Face
		North Peak of Mt. Index, East Face
V	None identified at this time	Slesse Peak, North Face
		Mt. Baring, North Face
		Liberty Bell, Liberty Crack Route
VI	None identified at this time	None identified at this time

OLYMPICS	CASCADES
1 Mt. Townsend Sentinel Peak Mt. Lena Mt. Buckhorn, Southwest Peak	Plummer Peak Yakima Peak Winchester Mountain Mt. Snoqualmie, easiest route

2   Mt. Ellinor, Route 1 (low in
    class)
Mt. Angeles, Route 1
Mt. Carrie (from Heart Lake)
Mt. Lincoln, Route 1
	Mt. Si, easiest route (low in
	    class)
	Silver Peak
	The Castle (easiest route)
	McClellan's Butte

3   Mt. Washington, Route 1 (low
    in class)
The Brothers, Route 1 (low in
    class)
Mt. Olympus, Route 1
Mt. Constance, Route 1
The Fin, Route 2
West Peak (Anderson Massif)
    Route 1 (high in class)
	Chair Peak, easiest route &
	    NE Arête
	Mt. Rainier, Emmons,
	    Gibraltar, and Ingraham
	    Routes
	Little Big Chief, easiest route
	Forbidden Peak, easiest route

4   Inner Constance, Route 1
    (low in class)
Mt. Johnson, Route 1
Chimney Peak, Route 2
Mt. Mathias, Route 1
The Horn, Route 1 (high in
    class)
	Mt. Stuart, West Ridge (low
	    in class)
	Magic Mountain, East Ridge
	Mixup Peak, East Face
	The Tooth, South Face
	Nooksack Tower (high in
	    class)

This is where the average party begins to use pitons.

5.0	The Bandersnatch
	Castle Spires, Route 3, West
	    Face
		Dinosaur Tower, Skyline
		    Route

5.2	Sweat Spire The Fin, Route 4	
5.3	The Royal Shaft Tran Spire	Castle Rock, Sabre Route

5.4	Mt. Constance, Route 2, West Arête Mt. Cruiser, Route 1–V	Castle Rock, Midway Route
5.5	Mt. Cruiser, Route 4, West Face The Horn, Route 2, West Face	Trigger Finger Liberty Bell, Beckey Route
5.6	The Arrowhead Mt. Cruiser, Route 3, NE Face	Castle Rock, Cat Burglar Route
5.7	Mt. Cruiser, Route 5, East Face Mt. Cruiser, Route 2, WSW Corner	Castle Rock, Canary and Angel Routes Chumstick Snag
5.8	None identified at this time	Grand Central Tower, Corkscrew Route Castle Rock, Damnation Crack
5.9	None identified at this time	Snow Creek Wall, Outer Space Route Castle Rock, Idiot's Delight Overhang
5.10	None identified at this time	Midnight Rock, Easter Overhang

Recommended Climbs

The following climbs are representative of the best that the Olympic Mountains have to offer. While not necessarily the longest, the highest, or the most difficult, they provide a typical cross-section of the types of climbing available, and are generally enjoyable and worthwhile.

One-Day Climbs

The Horn. A short but excellent rock climb on pillow lava in the scenic Sawtooth Ridge above Flapjack Lakes. A choice of routes is available.

Mt. Ellinor. Popular in any season, this short climb, mostly on good trail, is readily accessible and offers an excellent view of the interior.

Mt. Lincoln. A steep trail, followed by brush, scree, and a pleasant rock scramble, leads to a summit with a good view of the Sawtooth Ridge.

Mt. Stone. This scenic climb provides enough elevation gain to give a feeling of accomplishment and an excellent view of the interior.

Mt. Washington. One of the most popular summits in the range. Washington has a variety of routes, some quite challenging, and good mixed climbing in season.

Two-Day Climbs

The Brothers. A popular scenic climb in the eastern front range. Not difficult. The traverse is an excellent route in early season.

Mt. Constance. Even the "dog routes" are challenging, the summit is high, the scenery is superb, and the tough routes (3 or more days) are the most difficult in the range.

Cruiser. The Olympic's best-known and most frequently done rock climb, on excellent Sawtooth pillow lava. The summit is airy, the tough routes are hairy.

Warrior. Infrequently done, this peak deserves more attention for both beauty and climbing enjoyment.

Climbs of Three or More Days

Mt. Anderson. Located in the geographic and hydrographic center of the Olympics, this scenic glaciated peak reminds one of a miniature "major."

Mt. Mathias. Perhaps the least known of the more difficult peaks in the Olympics, Mathias is challenging by either route, and provides good mixed climbing.

The Needles. A visit to Royal Basin, in the protection of the rain shadow, is a must for those who would know the Olympics. Mt. Clark is the best climb, but Johnson, The Incisor, and Arrowhead are all worthwhile.

Mt. Olympus. The monarch of the range, Olympus can be a pleasant glaciated climb in good weather, or a nightmare of

Aerial View of Warrior Looking West (George W. Martin)

routefinding problems and crevasses in fog or sleet. The scenery is superb.

Winter Mountaineering

Winter mountaineering, an increasingly popular sport, can be enjoyed in the Olympics as well as in other ranges. The normal winter climbing season is December through March. Winter temperatures, influenced by the offshore flow of warm and moisture-laden air from the nearby Pacific, fluctuate with a freezing level ranging from 2000 to 6000 feet. This moderate weather contributes an abundance of mixed rain and snow. The climber's foremost problem is staying dry. Spare clothing, a necessity, should be double-wrapped in plastic or otherwise protected.

Avalanches are the greatest hazard in this range in the winter. Olympic snowfalls have high water content, even without the addition of occasional rainfall, and the combination increases the potential danger. Narrow ridges, heavily corniced, discourage passage, so the winter traveler must exercise caution in the gullies and couloirs. Some narrow valleys are the scene of tremendous avalanche activity, wherein the slopes of two opposing mountains each add their share to the destruction below. However, the peaks tend to unload their burdens in the first day of sunshine following a storm, and the climber can then proceed with the same care as is usually exercised in spring climbing.

Heavy snowfall makes the approaches for summit attempts inordinately long in most years. The winter climber may find his entire weekend spent snowshoeing over dreary miles of logging roads. The increasing use of snowmobiles has brought many Olympic summits within reach in winter, but users of these noisy beasts should carry snowshoes and emergency gear in case of mechnical breakdown. Snowslide areas, compacted and icy, present tricky traverses for the snowmobile. Be prepared for a hasty retreat if your car is in danger of being snowed in.

A listing of feasible winter climbs which can be enjoyable under proper conditions follows:

Recommended Winter Climbs

Mt. Angeles, Routes 1 and 2. The easiest peak to approach, since the Hurricane Ridge road is kept open during the holiday season and on weekends through April 1st. Snowshoes or skis should be taken for the easy one-day ascent.

Mt. Ellinor, Route 1. The Big Creek logging road, with its southern exposure, makes this peak and Mt. Washington easily approachable. An overnight camp at the head of the Ellinor chute with a traverse to Mt. Washington provides an interesting weekend.

Mt. Washington, Route 1. Always a good climb, but avalanche hazard in the Big Creek snow basin is ever present. Many climbers try its slopes on Washington's Birthday.

Copper Mountain. Though a long one-day trip, the views from this minor summit make the ascent worthwhile.

Mt. Pershing, Route 3. A two-day trip. The blanket of snow eliminates the brush found on this peak in the summer. The valley between Pershing and Washington should be avoided during avalanche conditions.

Mt. Thorson, Route 1. A one-day trip to the east summit. The climb can be continued via a very interesting ridge traverse to the main peak.

Mt. Stone, Route 1. If road conditions allow, this peak can be climbed in one long day.

Mt. Skokomish, Route 1. Beautiful, but notorious for avalanches. The many false summits cause frustration in foggy conditions.

The Brothers, Route 1. Avalanche conditions must be considered up the long steep gully on this two-day trip.

Warrior Peak. This beautiful climb has been done in two days when the road is open, but three would be more enjoyable.

Mt. Lincoln, Route 1. If the road is open, this is a one-day climb with minimum avalanche hazard.

Tyler Peak. A one-day climb if good conditions allow, with little avalanche hazard and a splendid view.

Mt. Townsend. A good one-day climb if snowmobiles are available for the logging road approach. The view is magnificent.

Mt. Walkinshaw. This is a fine two-day climb in the northern Needles, if the road is open.

Many of the peaks in the interior have been climbed in winter by experienced mountaineers on extended cross-country ski or snowshoe trips. Mt. Constance and Mt. Olympus have been ascended in winter by strong parties in years when conditions were optimum.

CLIMBING ROUTES

Sawtooth Ridge from Camp at Flapjack Lakes (Dave Sicks)

Skokomish-Duckabush Group

The southern mountains of the eastern Olympics are deeply dissected by three rivers flowing into Hood Canal: the Hamma Hamma, the Duckabush, and the North and South Forks of the Skokomish. Above Lake Cushman the North Fork of the Skokomish River flows south from its sources which, along with the Duckabush River, form a natural boundary virtually enclosing this group. West of the North Fork Skokomish River drainage, water flows into the Quinault River on its way to the Pacific Ocean.

While the general peak elevation is less than that of other parts of the Olympics, the contours are no less rugged. Near timberline, many lakes are nestled in parklike meadows and heather. Active glaciers have vanished long ago, but large snowfields persist on northern slopes all summer. The jagged Sawtooth Ridge just east of Flapjack Lakes has a number of prominent pillow-lava rock pinnacles, offering some top challenges for rock climbers.

Its proximity to metropolitan areas, with generally good climbing terrain and relatively accessible peaks, make this group by far the most frequently climbed in the Olympic Range.

Approaches

1. Skokomish River, (North Fork): This approach provides entrance to Lake Cushman and the beautiful Staircase area of the Olympic National Park. The Sawtooth Ridge, Mt. Steel, Mt. Lincoln, and Copper Mountain are the main peaks accessible from the Staircase area. This approach also leads to Lightning

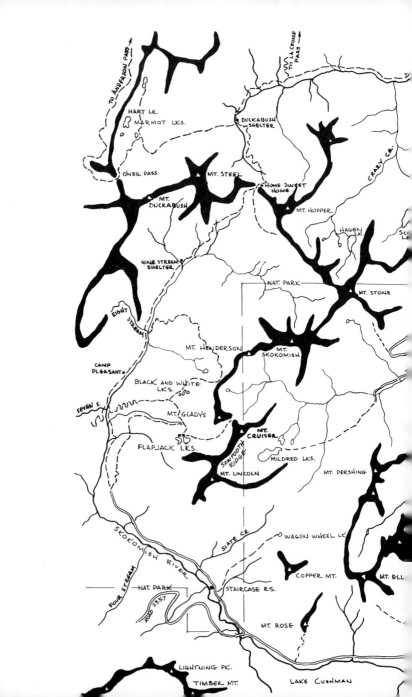

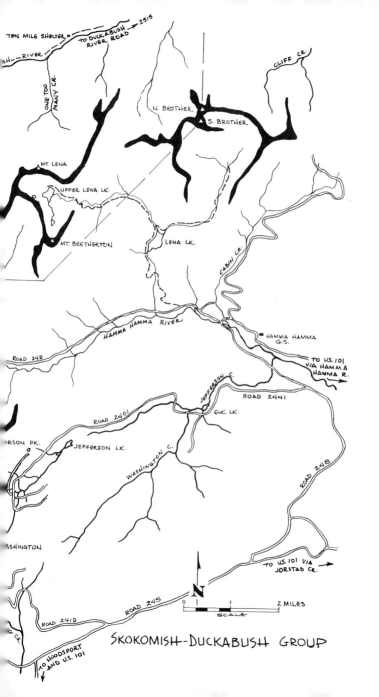

TEN MILE SHELTER
TO DUCKABUSH RIVER ROAD → 2515
~SH—RIVER
ONE TOO MANY CR.
CLIFF CR.
N. BROTHER
S. BROTHER
MT. LENA
UPPER LENA LK.
MT. BRETHERTON
LENA LK.
CABIN CR.
HAMMA HAMMA RIVER
HAMMA HAMMA G.S.
ROAD 248
TO U.S. 101 VIA HAMMA HAMMA R.
JEFFERSON C.
ROAD 2441
ROAD 2401
ELK LK.
~RSON PK.
JEFFERSON LK.
WASHINGTON C.
ROAD 2418
~ASHINGTON
TO U.S. 101 VIA JORSTAD CR.
N
0   1   2 MILES
SCALE
ROAD 245
ROAD 2419
~ CR.
TO HOODSPORT AND U.S. 101

SKOKOMISH-DUCKABUSH GROUP

Peak and the eastern climbing routes of Mt. Ellinor and Mt. Washington.

Two roads lead into this area from U.S. 101 on Hood Canal: the Lake Cushman road (a paved road from Hoodsport), and the Jorstad Creek road.

1a. The Lake Cushman road leaves U.S. 101 at Hoodsport (16 miles N of Shelton). Drive W on paved road for 9 miles to the "T" intersection with Forest Service road #245. Turn left and continue 6½ miles past the lake to the Staircase Ranger Station (770 ft.) in Olympic National Park.

A fairly good gravel road continues up river for 3.8 miles past the Staircase Ranger Station. At the end of the road (1492 ft.), several enjoyable trails wind into the Olympics. The most popular is the Skokomish River trail, which follows the river and then climbs to First Divide (9.1 miles, 4688 ft.) where it connects with the Duckabush River trail. Shelters are at Camp Pleasant (2.9 miles, 1530 ft.), Nine Stream (5.8 miles, 2090 ft.), and Home Sweet Home (9.4 miles, 4200 ft.).

Two other trails branch off the Skokomish River trail. The one to Black and White Lakes (4500 ft.) and Smith Lakes (3900 ft.) leaves the main trail 1.8 miles from the road end. The Six Ridge trail, which may be followed to the Quinault River, leaves the Skokomish River trail after it crosses the river (2 miles from the road end).

The Flapjack Lakes trail starts about 100 yards before the end of the road, extends 4.5 miles to Flapjack Lakes (3900 ft., 2 shelters) and then continues 1.5 miles to Gladys Divide, the starting point for many climbs in the Sawtooth Ridge including Mt. Cruiser.

1b. The Jorstad Creek road leaves U.S. 101 2 miles S of Eldon (at a log dump on Hood Canal). The road becomes Forest Service road #245 after 1.2 miles, and it connects with the Lake Cushman road in another 7.3 miles.

The Big Creek logging road, #2419 (used for the eastern approaches to Mt. Ellinor and Mt. Washington), branches from the Jorstad Creek road (#245) 7 miles from U.S. 101. This road can also be easily reached by turning right at the "T" intersection of the Lake Cushman road with road #245. Drive 1.5 miles more and turn hard left at the "Y."

2. Hamma Hamma River: Though one of the shorter rivers of the Olympics, the Hamma Hamma River flows through a scenic subalpine region. Its waters, flowing from many peaks including The Brothers, Mt. Stone, Mt. Skokomish, and Mt. Bretherton, are augmented by Jefferson Creek, the principal drainage of Mt. Washington and Mt. Pershing. All of those peaks except Mt. Washington are best reached via this approach. Like the Skokomish, this area may be reached by two roads.

2a. The Hamma Hamma River road (Forest Service road #249) branches W from U.S. 101 13½ miles N of Hoodsport. The Hamma Hamma Campground is reached after 6 miles. The road continues ½ mile to a junction with road #248, turns right, and then gradually climbs for 7 miles to where it crosses the Hamma Hamma River and immediately ends in a parking area. A trail leads from here to Mildred Lakes and the western approaches to Mt. Pershing.

The popular Lena Lakes trail begins on this road 7.7 miles from U.S. 101. Lower Lena Lake (1800 ft., 1 shelter) is reached after 3 miles of well-graded trail; the trail then continues 4 miles to Upper Lena Lake (4600 ft.). For the standard climbs of The Brothers, cross Lena Creek at the head of Lower Lena Lake and proceed up the East Fork Lena Creek through the "Valley of Silent Men."

2b. The Jorstad Creek road leaves U.S. 101 2 miles S of Eldon (at a log dump on Hood Canal). After 1.2 miles, the road forks. The right fork (#248) continues for 8.9 miles where it connects with the Hamma Hamma River road (#249) after crossing the river.

The Jefferson Creek road, used for the N and W approaches to Mt. Washington and the E and S approaches to the Pershing-Thorson Massif, is reached by turning left off road #248 about 6.5 miles from U.S. 101. Follow the Washington Creek road (#2441) for 3 miles and hold to the right on the Jefferson Creek road (#2401). Jefferson Lake is 3 miles farther.

3. Duckabush River: The 7-mile Duckabush River road begins just N of the Duckabush River bridge on U.S. 101 (22 miles N of Hoodsport and 2 miles S of Brinnon). In about 4 miles it becomes Forest Service road #2515, and at about 6 miles it turns left and becomes the Murhut Creek road (#2530). At this point, logging spur #2515A continues up river about a mile to the saddle (850 ft.) above Little Hump. This road, though rocky, is passable. From here, the Duckabush River trail climbs steeply over Big Hump and then follows the river, eventually connecting with the Skokomish River trail (16.5 miles, 2695 ft.). Trail shelters are located at Tenmile (9.3 miles, 1500 ft.), Upper Duckabush (16.3 miles, 2695 ft.), Marmot Lakes (19.9 miles, 4300 ft.), and Hart Lake (20.4 miles, 4800 ft.).

4. Quinault River: This approach, the primary entrance to the Southwestern Group, page 146, is seldom used for peaks in the southeastern Olympics. However, it does connect with several trails on the S edge of this group.

The Quinault River road leaves U.S. 101 ½ mile SE of Amanda Park near Lake Quinault and extends easterly for 21.6 miles (see Southwestern Group, page 148, for details). From just above the Graves Creek Campground (19.3 miles from U.S. 101), a 7.5-mile trail goes to Lake Sundown (3800 ft., 1 shelter). Near Lake Sundown, the trail forks, with one branch continuing to Six Ridge and the North Fork of the Skokomish River. The other branch climbs to Sundown Pass (4103 ft.), and then descends the South Fork Skokomish River. Lake Sundown may also be reached from the Wynoochee River road (#2312) via an unmaintained trail.

Ranger Stations: Hoodsport (just off U.S. 101), Staircase (Lake Cushman-Staircase road), Graves Creek (Quinault River road). Guard Stations: Hamma Hamma (Hamma Hamma River road), Interrorem (Duckabush River road).

Campgrounds: U.S. 101: Potlatch State Park, el. 20 ft. (3 miles S of Hoodsport).
Lake Cushman-Staircase Road: Lake Cushman State Park, el. 800 ft. (7 miles W of Hoodsport); Staircase, el. 850 ft. (16 miles W of Hoodsport).
Hamma Hamma River Road: Hamma Hamma, el. 600 ft. (6 miles W of U.S. 101); Lena Creek, el. 600 ft. (7.8 miles W of U.S. 101).

Duckabush River Road: Camp Collins, el. 200 ft. (4.1 miles W of U.S. 101).

Quinault River Road: Graves Creek Campground, el. 600 ft. (19 miles E of U.S. 101).

Wynoochee River Road: Wynoochee Falls, el. 1000 ft. (43 miles N of Montesano).

Vantage Points: Mt. Ellinor, Jefferson Ridge LO, and Mt. Jupiter are accessible by trail. An impressive closeup view of Mt. Washington, Mt. Pershing, Thorson Peak, and Mt. Stone may be seen by continuing up road #2401 past Jefferson Lake to a lookout point high on the E side of the Jefferson Creek valley.

Maps: Olympic National Forest; USGS 30-minute Olympic National Park and Vicinity; *The Olympics in Relief,* published by Richard A. Pargeter and George W. Martin; the following USGS 15-minute quadrangles: The Brothers, Mt. Steel, Mt. Christie, Mt. Tebo, and Grisdale.

THE BROTHERS   6866

This double-summited peak, the most imposing feature of the eastern skyline of the Olympics, is located 2 miles north of Lower Lena Lake on the Duckabush-Hamma Hamma River divide. It was named after the Fauntleroy brothers in 1856 by Professor George Davidson.

First ascent of the South Peak 1912 by T. Collier, O. Corkenill, W. Dehn, W. Fish, E. Goldsmith, and H. Trumbull. First ascent of the slightly lower North Peak 1908 by C. Hill and W. Hill via Cliff Creek (very brushy).

SOUTH PEAK   6866

ROUTE 1 (SOUTH COULOIR). I, 3. Follow the Lena Lake trail (leaves Hamma Hamma River road 7.7 miles from U.S. 101, 685 ft.) 3 miles to Lower Lena Lake (1800 ft., 1 shelter). Continue on trail around the head of the lake and up the East Fork of Lena Creek to where it branches (ca. 3 miles, 3000 ft.). Several good campsites are in the vicinity. From here, follow a faint trail in the general NW direction of the left (W) fork of the

The Brothers from the Northeast (George W. Martin)

creek. In ca. 30 minutes, a small avalanche meadow just below the first cliffs is reached. Cross the meadow and ascend W across a minor tree-covered ridge to a rocky or snow-filled gully. Climb this gully which opens into a second meadow. Ascend to the head of the meadow where it is best to climb a short distance right (E) via adjoining rock ledges to avoid minor cliffs. Next, climb ca. 200 yards and then bear slightly left (N) into the upper couloir which leads to the summit rocks. Time: 7 hours from road.

ROUTE 2. I, 4. From the lower meadow of Route 1, climb the cliffs directly to the E ridge, which leads to the summit. The upper part of the route is steep and exposed. Time: 8 hours from road.

ROUTE 3 (SW RIDGE). II, 3. Climb after an approach via the lower half of the Upper Lena Lake trail and a difficult brush crash to the Lena Peak-Brothers saddle. This, the early popular route, is very long. Time: 9 hours from saddle.

NORTH PEAK   ca. 6800

ROUTE 1. II, 3. After reaching approximately the 6000-ft. level of Route 1, South Peak, contour around into the eastern "Great Basin." An alternate route is to descend from the South Peak summit into the same basin, dropping below the prominent buttress. From the basin, ascend a couloir and moderate rock to the small summit. Time: 9 hours from camp at Lena Creek forks.

ROUTE 2. II, 3. This route should be done in early season because of later heavy brush. Continue up the far right branch of Lena Creek past the turnoff for Route 1, South Peak. Near the upper end of the valley, turn up into the eastern "Great Basin." From the basin, use either the snow couloir of Route 1 or make an ascending traverse around to the N slope of the peak, and proceed up the N ridge to the summit. Time: 9 hours from camp at Lena Creek forks.

ROUTE 3. II, 4. First ascent 1970 by R. Beckett, H. Pinsch, L. Triboulet, and R. Yekel.
Take the Murhut Creek logging road (see Duckabush River approach) to where it reaches the saddle between Cabin Creek and the E fork of Cliff Creek (ca. 4100 ft.). Ascend wooded ridge W and S until reaching a narrow rocky ridge (ca. 30 minutes)

which extends all the way W to the summit. At ca. 4900 ft., the ridge's gendarmes may be bypassed by crossing to the N side and traversing to the meadow on the N slopes of the peak. Continue as in Route 2. Time: 10 hours from road; 10 hours down.

BROTHERS TRAVERSE: An interesting traverse can be made from either summit to the other.

MT. LENA (MT. BALDY)   5995
Located ½ mile north of Upper Lena Lake.
ROUTE. I, 1. From Lower Lena Lake, proceed on the trail 4 miles to Upper Lena Lake (ca. 4500 ft.). Walk N and W up easy slopes to the top. Time: 6 hours from road.

MT. BRETHERTON   5960
An elongated double-summited peak located 1 mile south of Upper Lena Lake.
ROUTE 1. I, 2. From Upper Lena Lake proceed S past Milk Lake and ascend the higher (S) summit via a saddle and upper basin traverse. As an alternate route from Upper Lena Lake, ascend the N ridge and cross the N summit to the higher S summit. Time: 2 hours from Upper Lena Lake.
ROUTE 2. I, 2. Follow the logging road which leaves the Hamma Hamma road between Boulder and Whitehorse Creeks N to where it crosses Boulder Creek. Ascend E to the top of the ridge and follow it N to the summit. Allow a full day for this climb.

MT. STONE   6612
A sharp, multiple-peaked mountain located at the head of the Skokomish River, Crazy Creek, and Whitehorse Creek; it has several permanent snowfields on the north and west faces.

SOUTH PEAK   6612
ROUTE 1. I, 2. At 12.1 miles from U.S. 101 on the Hamma Hamma River road (0.2 mile past Boulder Creek bridge), turn right on a logging road and drive 1.3 miles. Park car at the

second switchback (ca. 2500 ft.) and find the trail about 100 yards up the road on the left side high on a cut above the road. Follow trail W until a way trail branches to the right (N) just short of Whitehorse Creek. Follow way trail northerly into a small meadow. Continue on the right side of the meadow to a slight headwall which may be ascended up the right side of a small gully. Climb northwesterly up rock and scree slopes, keeping the ridge with its terminating large buttress on the right (E). The W ridge, when reached, may be followed E to the summit, which involves a rock scramble. A ledge system on the left (N) of the summit block simplifies a winter ascent. Time: 5 hours from road.

ROUTE 2. I, 2. Follow the logging road of Route 1 until it crosses a small creek (2.3 miles, ca. 3300 ft.). Climb W along the creekbed through timber and brush for about 1000 ft. Continue upward to a notch in the SE ridge of Mt. Stone, known as St. Peter's Gate (ca. 5900 ft.). Proceed through the notch and join Route 1. Time: 5 hours from road.

ROUTE 3. I, 2. From First Divide take the Mt. Hopper way trail to the saddle S of Mt. Hopper and then follow the ridge SE about 2 miles to the saddle S of Hagen Lakes. From here, climb E up snowfields to the base of the summit tower.

MIDDLE PEAK   ca. 6600
First ascent 1932 by C. Ullin and party.

ROUTE 1. I, 2. Follow Route 1, South Peak, to the notch (ca. 5900 ft.) on the SE ridge of Mt. Stone. Pass easterly through this notch (known as St. Peter's Gate). Contour N on snowfields or heather to a Y-shaped couloir. Ascend the right branch to the summit gendarmes. Make the final ascent on the N via rocky ledges. Though the South Peak is slightly higher, there are registers on both peaks. Time: 7 hours from road.

ROUTE 2. I, 2. From Hagen Lakes, climb S up scree or snow and rock to the summit gendarmes.

NORTH PEAK   ca. 6400
First ascent 1935 by T. Martin, C. Ullin and party.

ROUTE 1. I, 2. Traverse from the Middle Peak via the rocky connecting ridge.

ROUTE 2. I, 2. From the Scout Lake way trail, ascend SW over talus or snow to a prominent pass in the long ridge N of the North Peak. A long traverse over and around the gendarmes of the N ridge leads to the summit.

THE BANDERSNATCH   ca. 5300

This 150-ft. spire is east of the north ridge of Mt. Stone (Jabberwocky Ridge) and is prominently visible to the north from the small lakes east of Mt. Stone.

First ascent 1958 by D. N. Anderson, J. Richardson, and E. Rodgers.

ROUTE. I, 5.0. Approach the spire from the small lakes (4600 ft.) at the E base of Mt. Stone. A rising traverse to the N ascends to the spire's SW base. A chimney leads to a platform below the notch between the two summits. Traverse past a tree to a belay point behind a big rock. The last pitch is an 80-ft. high-angle lead protected by a piton. The rappel rope should be tied to the tree before ascending, and stretched across the top.

MT. SKOKOMISH   6434

A rather massive peak on the Skokomish-Hamma Hamma River divide. There are 3 summits; the highest is the south peak.

ROUTE 1. I, 2. Follow description of Route 1, Mt. Stone, until reaching the small meadow. Continue westerly until past the Lake of the Angels (4800 ft.). Climb southwesterly on ridges and benches to the shoulder of Mt. Skokomish. Continue to a snowfield on the SE side. Make a slight descent to the SW, turn right, and ascend over rock and brush to the summit. Time: 5 hours from road.

ROUTE 2. I, 2. From Flapjack Lakes and Gladys Divide (5000 ft.), traverse 2½ miles northerly past Mt. Henderson to the summit. Perhaps faster than this ridge traverse would be descent to the N of Gladys Divide followed by a direct ascent up the peak.

This route has also been followed from above Smith Lake after an approach via the Black and White Lakes trail.

MT. HENDERSON   ca. 6000

Located nearly a mile southwest of Mt. Skokomish and 1½ miles north-northeast of Mt. Gladys.

ROUTE. I, 1. An ascent may be made either from Mt. Gladys or from above Smith Lake after an approach via the Black and White Lakes trail.

PERSHING MASSIF   6154

A group of rock summits located between the Hamma Hamma River and Jefferson Creek, 1¼ miles north-northwest of Mt. Washington. Approach can be made via the Jefferson Creek road (#2401) or the Hamma Hamma River road (#249). See Hamma Hamma River approach for details.

MT. PERSHING (SOUTH PEAK)   6154

First ascent 1939 by D. Dooley, R. Henderson, W. Ingalls, and R. Mandelhorn via Route 4.

ROUTE 1. II, 3. First ascent 1966 by A. Bloomer, R. Etten, and K. Spencer.

Leave the Jefferson Creek road (#2401) 2 miles past Jefferson Lake at the intersection of a side road from the W (ca. 2500 ft.). Follow the side road for ca. 75 yards. Leave the road and contour through timber just above the E and S sides of an extensive marshy area to an avalanche basin beneath Mt. Washington's NE cliffs (30 minutes). Next, climb westerly under the cliffs on the N side of Mt. Washington, staying high along the SE side of the valley to avoid heavy brush. After passing two wooded sections and an avalanche slope, cross the valley just above a large scree slide which lies under the cliffs of Mt. Pershing's S ridge. Continue up the valley to the Lake Ellinor cirque, with its gigantic overhanging rock (ca. 2 hours from road, 3900 ft.). Turn hard right and climb N ¼ mile to a low spot in Pershing's S ridge (5450 ft.). Descend slightly on the W side of the ridge and contour N far enough to bypass Mt. Ben (a minor summit on the S ridge, 5650 ft.). Next, climb ledges, snow, and easy rock to the ridge crest and then follow the narrow exposed arête to the summit. Time: 8 hours from road.

ROUTE 2. II, 4. First ascent 1967 by H. Pinsch, B. West, and M. West.

Leave the Jefferson Creek road (#2401) as in Route 1. Travel W through the jungle past the right side of a small lake formed by Jefferson Creek. Continue westerly up a broad couloir to a narrow bench (ca. 5200 ft.) keeping the S ridge of Mt. Pershing directly on the left. Contour N and into another couloir, cross the head of this couloir to the N side and ascend left (W) to the narrow, exposed ridge of Route 1. Continue on to the summit. Time: 8 hours from road.

Mt. Ben (ca. 5650) may be ascended by continuing past the bench in the first couloir to the ridge crest. Climb the open-book of a small pinnacle, or contour to the left of the base. Continue N on easy rock to a short chimney which ends at the summit. One may descend N and continue on to the summit of Mt. Pershing from here.

ROUTE 3 (EAST RIDGE). II, 3. First ascent 1959 by D. Bechlem, J. Christiansen, R. Etten, and R. Wood.

Using the approach of Route 1, continue up the side road for 0.6 mile to where the road contours the E end of Mt. Pershing's E ridge. Climb westerly to the ridge crest and then travel W along the S side of the timbered crest to ca. 5000 ft. The summit can be seen to the W from this point. Descend about 300 ft. into a basin and proceed W toward the summit. Ascend the E side of the S ridge of Pershing via an obvious snow gully and follow the narrow exposed ridge of Route 1 to the top. Time: 8 hours from road.

ROUTE 4. II, 3. From the end of the Hamma Hamma River road (#249) where it has crossed the river, take the Mildred Lakes trail for ca. 2 miles or to where the trail recrosses the creek. Leave the trail and climb SE over scree to a point just S of cliffs of the Middle Peak. Next, climb E to the saddle between the Middle and South Peaks. From here, the main summit can be reached either by moderate rock scrambling on the right hand ridge, or by way of a more difficult rock gully directly left of the ridge. Time: 8 hours from road.

ROUTE 5. II, 3. First ascent 1952 by A. Filion and J. Murray.

Leave the Hamma Hamma River road (#249) at the Boulder

Creek bridge (ca. 5 miles above its junction with road #248). Cross the river via a log jam and proceed S up the gully on the hillside through brush, scree, and over snow (early in the season) to a basin at ca. 4000 ft. Continue climbing to the head of the basin, and then cross the 5000-ft. pass in the N ridge of Thorson Peak. Drop slightly and contour westerly along the NW side of the Pershing-Thorson ridge. Climb to the saddle (5600 ft.) between the South and Middle Peaks, and continue S to the summit as in Route 4. Time: 8 hours from road.

ROUTE 6. II, 3. Drive 6.6 miles up the Hamma Hamma River road (#249) from its intersection with road #248, or about a mile past Boulder Creek. Walk toward the river, to an old logging road. Follow the logging road until it meets the river. Cross on any available logs. Follow S through brush, then SE along the right side of the creek bed, reaching a basin at 4000 ft. Continue southerly and somewhat to the right, reaching a second basin at ca. 5000 ft. Proceed up this basin to the Middle-South Peak saddle (5600 ft.). Traverse left to the rocky ridge running E to the summit. This route is quite brushy. Time: 7 hours from road.

MIDDLE PEAK   ca. 5800
First ascent 1951 by A. Filion, N. Jacques, J. Murray, and K. Spencer via Route 2.

ROUTE 1. I, 2. Climb from the South-Middle Peak saddle after an approach via Route 4, South Peak. Time: 6 hours from road.

ROUTE 2. I, 3. Use the approach of Route 4, South Peak, until under the obvious cliffs of the Middle Peak (ca. 1½ hours from road). Climb these cliffs directly, generally following the line of easiest passage to the summit. Time: 5 hours from road.

NORTH PEAK   ca. 5600
ROUTE. I, 3. From the end of the Hamma Hamma River road, take the Mildred Lakes trail ca. ½ mile to where it switches back. From this point, climb SSE over brush and scree to the base of the cliffs of the North Peak. Climb E under these cliffs around to the SE side of the peak. From here, the final 200 ft. is over steep but pleasant rock. Time: 5 hours from road.

THORSON PEAK ca. 5700

Located between Jefferson Creek and the Hamma Hamma River, 1½ miles northeast of Mt. Pershing. Named for R. Thorson, who lost his life on The Brothers in 1948.

First ascent 1958 by D. N. Anderson, R. Oram, R. Peterson, and K. Spencer via Route 2.

ROUTE 1. I, 3. First ascent 1962 by A. Bloomer, D. Butler, A. Filion, J. Horn, R. Harniss, R. Oram, J. Pinsch, and K. Spencer.

Follow the side road of Routes 1, 2, and 3 of Mt. Pershing ca. 1 mile just past a small creek. Ascend steep hillside W through timber to an open meadow of gigantic boulders. Bear slightly to the right, up scree or snow slopes and onto the ridge. Follow this ridge past the lower (E) summit ¼ mile SW to the top.

As an alternate route, instead of ascending scree slope above the boulder field, contour to left through a slide-alder patch, and climb W to a saddle on the ridge leading to Mt. Pershing. Ascend N and E up easy rock to the summit. Time: 4 hours from road.

ROUTE 2 (NORTH COULOIR). I, 3. Thorson Peak is the high point ahead and slightly to the left when entering the basin in Route 5, Mt. Pershing. From this basin, ascend the steep snow couloir on the left of the peak to the col on the ridge. From this col, turn right and climb easy rock to the summit. Time: 6 hours from road.

TRAN SPIRE ca. 4900

Located directly north of Thorson Peak.

First ascent 1958 by D. N. Anderson and R. Peterson.

ROUTE. I, 5.3. From the basin (4000 ft.) in Route 5, Mt. Pershing, walk E a short distance to the base of this prominent 250-ft. spire. Two long leads on the rotten rock of the SE wall gain a large ledge on the S corner. Here a stunted tree provides an anchor for the 130-ft. rappel necessary for the descent. From this point, the summit is easily reached. Several smaller towers in the area offer first ascents. Time: 6 hours from road.

MT. WASHINGTON 6255

This peak is the highest point on the rocky ridge overlooking Lake Cushman from the north, and is named for its resemblance

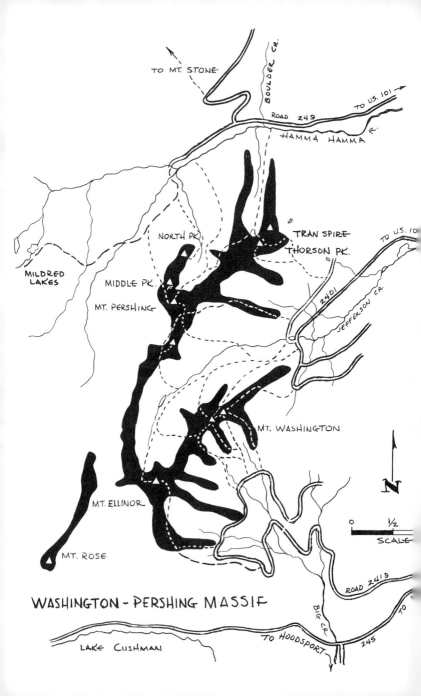

WASHINGTON - PERSHING MASSIF

to George Washington's profile. The "chin" is the summit. Due to easy access and variety of routes (snow and good rock) it is a popular peak among local climbers. In years of heavy snowfall, the steep slopes are prone to avalanches; early climbs should be undertaken with caution. East-side routes are approached from the Big Creek logging road (#2419). North- and west-side routes are approached from the Jefferson Creek road (#2401).

ROUTE 1-A. I, 3. Take the Big Creek logging road (#2419) for 6.5 miles to just short of its second crossing of Big Creek (wooden bridge below prominent waterfall, ca. 2800 ft.). Park car 100 yards S of Big Creek, and take the way trail leading westerly for 300 yards. Leave the trail and traverse N (right) through some brush into Big Creek above the waterfall. Follow Big Creek NW to a large basin (4500 ft.). Continue W up a steep snow slope with care around a bergschrund until the broad ridge stretching N is reached. Continue N to the summit block. The summit block may be climbed either directly up the rock or by contouring to the right on a rocky ledge and up the snow slope on the N side. Time: 4 hours from road.
Washington's "nose" NE of the summit is a short rock scramble. A group of rock pinnacles just below and to the left of Big Creek basin offer short but moderately difficult rock climbs.

ROUTE 1-B. I, 3. Continue past the second crossing of Big Creek for 0.3 mile to where timber starts. Ascend through trees to a rocky ridge. Climb this tree-covered ridge for about 200 ft. elevation gain, then contour left into Big Creek basin. Continue as in Route 1-A. Time: 4 hours from road.

ROUTE 2. I, 3. Continue past the second crossing of Big Creek, and ascend through trees as in Route 1-B. Where Route 1-B bears left, continue up the rocky ridge (staying somewhat to the right) to a large buttress (ca. 4500 ft.). Traverse N through a notch in a minor ridge, keeping the buttress on the left. Ascend directly W up steep snow slopes to the summit. Time: 4 hours from road.

ROUTE 3 (SOUTHEAST RIDGE). I, 4. When reaching the buttress of Route 2, climb on ledges to the crest of the ridge. Stay quite close to the crest, following the ridge westerly. Routefinding may be a problem, and two rappels are necessary to continue. Continue to the summit block where the ridge joins Route 1. Time: 6 hours from road.

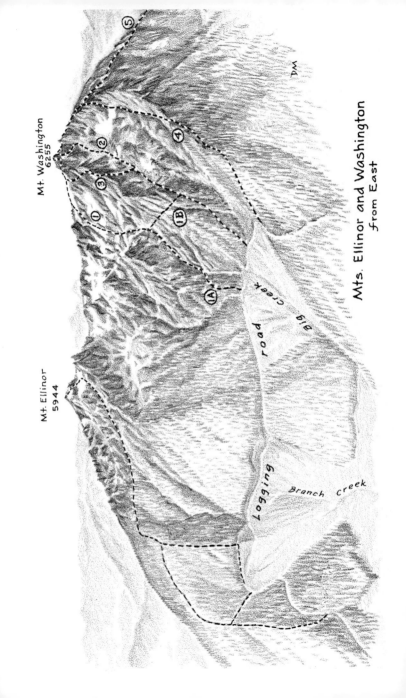

Mt. Washington
6255

Mt. Ellinor
5944

Mts. Ellinor and Washington
from East

Big Creek road

Branch Creek

Logging

ROUTE 4 (EAST RIDGE). I, 4. Continue on logging road ca. 0.6 mile past the second crossing of Big Creek (just past the crossing of the E fork of Big Creek) at ca. 3200 ft. Take the Mt. Washington trail, which leads N to Jefferson Pass, the saddle between the Big Creek and Jefferson Creek drainages (3850 ft.). Turn left (W) and continue to the base of the E ridge. Climb the steep wooded ridge which becomes rock and turns northward. Follow the narrow ridge crest, bypassing some of the gendarmes on the right to a huge buttress. This difficulty is overcome by traversing left into a large cirque. Follow the head of the cirque to a narrow gully with a 30-ft. chockstone. After climbing a wall to the left of the chockstone, take one of two choices: either proceed straight up the wall, or up another chockstone chimney. The regained ridge crest is broad and rounded all the way to the "nose." From here, a rappel or a short exposed descent leads to the summit. Time: 5 hours from road.

Reference: 1960 *Mazama*.

ROUTE 5 (NORTHEAST RIDGE). I, 3. First ascent 1964 by D. N. Anderson and L. Scott.

From where the Jefferson Creek road (#2401) doubles back to the E (ca. 2 miles past Jefferson Lake), leave the car and scramble SW up the hillside to the ridge crest overlooking the N face. Ascend the NE ridge, bypassing most of the buttresses on the left. The final scramble skirts the wall on the E face and ends atop the "nose." Continue to the summit as in Route 4. Time: 5 hours from road.

ROUTE 6 (NORTHEAST FACE). I, 3. First ascent 1959 by D. N. Anderson, A. Bloomer, R. Harniss, R. Hebble, N. Jacques, J. Koch, and K. Spencer.

Take the Jefferson Creek road (#2401) 2 miles past Jefferson Lake to the intersection of a side road from the W (ca. 2500 ft.). Follow the side road for ca. 75 yards. Contour through timber just above the E side of an extensive swampy area and on westerly to an avalanche basin beneath the NE cliffs (30 minutes). Ascend through the lower cliffs on their left side ca. 500 ft. to an upper basin; thence traverse right to the chute emptying over the lower cliffs. Ascend to the head of the chute and then climb directly to the obvious notch near the confluence of the NE and N ridges over steep snow or slab. From here, bear left to the summit of the "nose" and join Route 4. Time: 5 hours from road.

ROUTE 7 (NORTH-NORTHWEST FACE). I, 3. First ascent 1960 by D. N. Anderson, A. Bloomer, K. Heathershaw, J. Newman, and D. Blitz.

Approach as in Route 6. From the avalanche basin, contour SW just below the cliffs, crossing two wooded sections and one snow-and-slide-alder slope to a second snow slope. Ascend this ca. 500 ft. until a ledge allows a traverse left to avoid the cliffs above and below. Contour right, above the upper cliffs (5000 ft.) and continue until able to turn left. Thence climb directly up to either the "nose" or the summit. Time: 6 hours from road.

ROUTE 8 (SOUTHWEST SNOWFIELDS). II, 3. First ascent 1967 by D. Baker, R. Etten, G. Sinrud, and K. Spencer.

From a huge overhanging rock in the meadow just below Lake Ellinor (see Mt. Pershing, Route 1, for approach), proceed S past Lake Ellinor toward the head of the cirque. About ¼ mile S of the lake is a break in the eastern cliffs. Climb E through this break, then climb NE over snow or talus to the base of a broad couloir. Climb this couloir to the ridge saddle and a junction with Route 1 just below the summit. Time: 8 hours from road.

MT. ELLINOR   5944

The southernmost high peak of the ridge overlooking Lake Cushman from the north, named in 1856 after Ellinor Fauntle-roy of Seattle.

ROUTE 1. I, 2. Drive the Big Creek logging road (#2419) for 5.4 miles, 0.6 mile past the Mt. Ellinor trail, to where the road turns sharply N (2800 ft.). Take a fire trail on the W side of the road for 75 yards to a wooded hogback ridge. If early in the year before the road is open, leave the car at the first crossing of Big Creek (3.6 miles, 2200 ft.) and hike up a logged-over area, paralleling Branch Creek, to the hogback ridge. Climb the hogback to its junction with the Mt. Ellinor trail at just under 4000 ft.

As an alternate route, ascend a slight draw at the road's sharp turn and join the Mt. Ellinor trail at a point overlooking Lake Cushman. Follow the trail to the hogback.

From this junction, continue up the hogback through open woods to a point some 300 ft. above a large prominent rock (4000 ft.). Angle right, leaving the ridge and entering a small meadow. Across the meadow, an easy 1000-ft. chute leads to a basin about 250 ft. below and N of the summit. From the basin, bear slightly left to the summit. An interesting variation is to proceed up the hogback beyond the big rock to the S ridge of the mountain, and then follow this large ridge to the summit. Time: 3 hours from road.

ROUTE 2 (WEST ARÊTE). II, 3. First ascent 1967 by K. Jensen, R. Oram, G. Sinrud, and K. Spencer.
From the huge overhanging rock at the lower end of Lake Ellinor (see Mt. Pershing, Route 1, for approach), proceed S past the lake toward the head of the cirque. Ascend southerly over snow or talus slopes to a saddle, the lowest point in the sharp ridge running between Mt. Ellinor and Mt. Pershing (4½ hours from road). From the saddle, climb the ridge E over rock and snow. The only difficulty, a 200-ft. buttress, can be passed on the S via gullies and some interesting rock pitches. Time: 7 hours from road.

ELLINOR-WASHINGTON TRAVERSE. To accomplish this interesting traverse, descend the chute of Route 1 ca. 200 ft. and cross the ridge that forms the N side of the gully. Next, traverse a minor basin to Big Creek basin. Continue on to Washington's summit via Route 1, Mt. Washington. Time: 3 hours from Mt. Ellinor.
In the summer, this traverse offers a full day's climb by ascending the ridge at the *Horse's Mouth* formed by the intersection of the Ellinor ridge and Washington ridge. Either follow the ridge, crossing between the rock pinnacles, or (more interesting) stay on the ridge top.
The rock pinnacle at the head of the Mt. Ellinor chute, known as *"A" Peak*, offers a short rock scramble.

COPPER MOUNTAIN 5425
Located 2 miles west of Mt. Ellinor, this peak has some spectacular cornices in the spring.

ROUTE. I, 2. From the Staircase Ranger Station (900 ft.), take the 3-mile trail to Wagonwheel Lake (4100 ft.). From the lake, proceed S (right) up a wooded ridge, and contour left into the basin slightly NW of the peak. Climb directly to the E (highest) summit, or ascend to the right through a notch in the ridge with a S approach to the rocky top. Time: 6 hours from road.

LIGHTNING PEAK   4654
Located ca. 2 miles west of Lake Cushman, giving an excellent view of Sawtooth Ridge to the north.

ROUTE. I, 3. Turn left at the upper end of Lake Cushman onto road #2357. Drive for 3 miles and park car where Elk Creek crosses the road. Climb E through slash then timber ca. 1 mile before reaching a steep couloir on the right. Ascend the couloir and turn left to the rocky summit. Variation from this route can be made by climbing to the left of the couloir. Time: 4 hours from road.

SAWTOOTH RIDGE   6104
This ridge of sharp summits, for the most part solid rock, is known to local climbers as some of the best climbing in the Olympics. Its pillow-lava formations provide good handholds but few piton cracks, and a bolt kit should be carried by those venturing off established routes. The vertical pitches of this peculiar rock offer an interesting challenge for the experienced climber.
This popular climbing area is best approached from the west via the 4.1-mile trail to 3900-ft. Flapjack Lakes (a heavily-used camping area with a shortage of firewood) and its 1.5-mile continuation to Gladys Divide. Most of the following route descriptions start on the west side, at or above Flapjack Lakes. The major summits and pinnacles are listed starting at Mt. Lincoln on the south, and continuing northeast along the ridge to Noodle Needle. Exceptions to this pattern are clearly noted.

MT. LINCOLN   5868
Located on the Madeline Creek-Slate Creek Divide.
First ascent 1932 by K. Soult and F. Harmon.

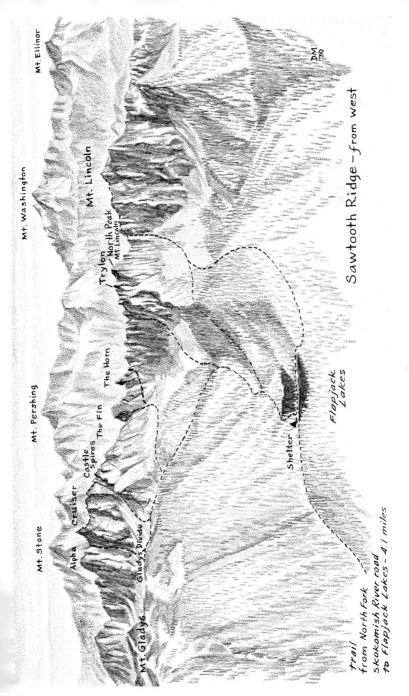

Mt. Ellinor

Mt. Washington

Mt. Lincoln

Trylon
North Peak
Mt. Lincoln

Mt. Pershing

The Horn

Mt. Stone

Alpha
Cruiser
Castle
Spires
The Fin

Gladys Divide

Mt. Gladys

Shelter

Flapjack
Lakes

DM
'70

Sawtooth Ridge — from west

trail
from North Fork
Skokomish River road
to Flapjack Lakes — 4.1 miles

ROUTE 1. I, 2. The Mt. Lincoln trail leaves the North Fork Skokomish River road 2.4 miles beyond the Staircase Ranger Station and continues NE 2½ miles to ca. 3300 ft. where it fades out. From the end of the trail, climb right (ENE) through an old brush-covered burn, and then directly up the open hillside to the right of the ridge crest. Pass to the E of the false summit, and continue on the moderate slope for ¼ mile to the summit. Time: 7 hours from the road.

ROUTE 2. I, 3. From Flapjack Lakes, either contour to the right around, or climb E and then S over, a forested ridge to the head of Madeline Creek basin. From here, some exposed rock scrambling leads to the N ridge. Follow this ridge to the summit. The prominent 5700-ft. N summit of Mt. Lincoln seen from the lakes should be kept to the left. Time: 3 hours from Flapjack Lakes.

ROUTE 3. I, 2. Cross to the E side of Sawtooth Ridge through the notch at the head of Harniss Chute. To reach Harniss Chute, leave the Gladys Divide trail ca. ¼ mile above Flapjack Lakes. Proceed through timber, soon reaching a small meadow. From here, a prominent rock slide marks the entrance of Harniss Chute. After reaching the ridge crest, descend the E side several hundred feet and contour S. Ascend the prominent couloir on Mt. Lincoln's ENE face. The lefthand peak is the summit. Time: 5 hours from Flapjack Lakes.

APPROACH NOTE: The following 5 gendarmes are best approached via Harniss Chute (see Route 3, Mt. Lincoln). They are described in order from the ridge notch SW towards the N peak of Mt. Lincoln.

THE CLEAVER AND SLAB TOWER

Each rock tower has a simple one-pitch ascent.

RECTAGON   ca. 5600

ROUTE. I, 4. Ascend a ledge leading around the NW face. At the end of the ledge, turn and climb the single pitch on down-sloping slab to the summit. Time: 4 hours from Flapjack Lakes.

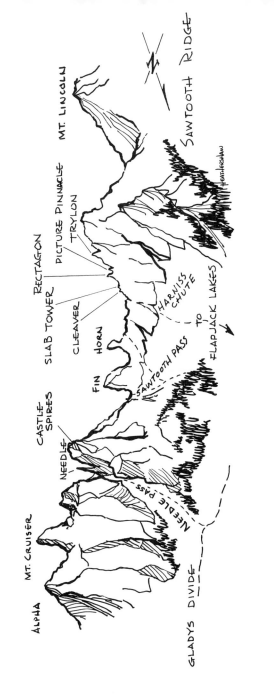

ALPHA

MT. CRUISER

CASTLE SPIRES

NEEDLE

NEEDLE PASS

GLADYS DIVIDE

FIN HORN

CLEAVER

SLAB TOWER

RECTAGON

PICTURE PINNACLE
TRYLON

MT. LINCOLN

SAWTOOTH RIDGE

HARNISS CHUTE

SAWTOOTH PASS

TO FLAPJACK LAKES

Heathersham

THE TRYLON   ca. 5700

A short three-sided gendarme seen prominently from Flapjack Lakes, located just north of the north summit of Mt. Lincoln.
First ascent 1941 by F. Beckey and H. Beckey.

ROUTE. I, 4. Climb the SE side with a tricky start from a high handhold. Time: 4 hours from Flapjack Lakes.

PICTURE PINNACLE   ca. 5650

A steep 100-ft. tower adjoining The Trylon on the east.
First ascent 1941 by F. Beckey and H. Beckey.

ROUTE. I, 4. Ascend a narrow chimney on the SE side.

APPROACH NOTE: The next two summits on this interesting ridge, The Fin and The Horn, are seen quite prominently from Flapjack Lakes. Although this is the lowest part of the ridge, some of the best Sawtooth climbs are on these two peaks. The easiest approach is to follow the Gladys Divide trail for ca. 1 mile above Flapjack Lakes to an open meadow on the right. Leave the trail and travel east, crossing a small rocky hump. The first narrow chute to the left of The Fin leads to a notch in the ridge, called Sawtooth Pass. For routes on The Horn, contour directly below the west face of The Fin to a ledge on the west side of The Horn.

THE FIN   ca. 5500

ROUTE 1. I, 2. Climb the gully to Sawtooth Pass (notch in ridge N of The Fin). Cross Sawtooth Pass and contour around to the E side. Climb easy rock to the summit. Time: 3 hours from Flapjack Lakes.

ROUTE 2. I, 3. Contour beneath the W face of The Fin to the notch in the ridge S of the peak. Climb directly up the exposed S ridge. Time: 3 hours from Flapjack Lakes.

ROUTE 3 (WEST FACE). I, 5.5. First ascent 1959 by D. N. Anderson and R. Harniss.

Leave the gully that leads to the S. ridge just below the notch and traverse left (N) about 40 ft. to the first break in the shallow overhang above. Climb up a superficial chimney, and traverse a few feet to the left. Climb the very strenuous crack (slightly overhanging) to an excellent belay behind a flake. Scramble

SMITH LK.

MURDOCK LKS.

BLACK & WHITE LKS.

MT. GLADYS △

GLADYS DIVIDE

AHUE CR.

TO OKOMISH RIVER RD.

NEEDLE PASS

ALPHA

MT. CRUISER

NEEDLE

CASTLE SPIRES

SAWTOOTH PASS

FIN

HORN

CLEAVER

SLAB TOWER

PICTURE PINNACLE

RECTAGON

FLAPJACK LKS.

TRYLON

MILDRED LAKES

ADELINE CR.

MT. LINCOLN

0   ½ MI.

SCALE

SAWTOOTH RIDGE

SLATE CR.

along the flake to a point where an easier section gives access to the notch a few feet S of the summit. The first pitch is quite difficult. Bring knife-blade pitons. Time: 3 hours from Flapjack Lakes.

ROUTE 4 (NORTHEAST FACE). I, 5.2. First ascent 1966 by H. Pinsch and G. Tate.
From about 50 ft. E of Sawtooth Pass, climb directly up the face for 30 ft. Make an ascending traverse to the left, to the base of a deep chimney. Two pitons and two runners were used in the first ascent for this long lead. Stem the chimney to its top, which is within 50 ft. of the summit. Time: 3 hours from Flapjack Lakes.

THE HORN   ca. 5500
First ascent 1940 by R. Carlow, D. Dooley, R. Henderson, E. Johnson, and V. Johnson.

ROUTE 1. I, 4. Contour beneath the W faces of The Fin and The Horn to the ridge notch S of the objective. Cross the ridge to the SE and climb an openbook with cannon hole, or a vertical chimney, to a platform 40 ft. below the top. From here, traverse to the right to a good belay spot, and then climb the nearly vertical E face. Time: 3 hours from Flapjack Lakes.
As an alternate route from the platform, climb the direct overhang or traverse to the left and up (5.3).

ROUTE 2 (WEST FACE). I, 5.5. Just before reaching the ridge notch of Route 1, turn left and climb up behind a small gendarme. From the ledge just N of the gendarme, climb directly up the W face to a secure belay point behind a flake. From here, either climb left to the summit or scramble to the right up to the platform of Route 1. Time: 3 hours from Flapjack Lakes.

APPROACH NOTE: The summits north of The Fin are commonly approached from Needle Pass. Needle Pass is at the head of the long snow finger visible from Gladys Divide.

CASTLE SPIRES   ca. 5800
This peak is the irregular mass between Sawtooth Pass and Needle Pass.

First ascent 1952 by N. Jacques, L. Nothwang, and D. Smith via Route 2.

ROUTE 1. I, 3. Scramble to the summit from Needle Pass.

ROUTE 2. I, 3. Ascend the couloir on the SE corner (from the E side of Sawtooth Pass) and scramble on exposed terrain to the highest of the gendarmes. As an alternate route, climb directly up the ridge from Sawtooth Pass.

ROUTE 3 (WEST FACE). I, 5.0. First ascent 1962 by A. Filion and K. Spencer.

From ¼ mile below Gladys Divide, climb to the lone green tree at the base of the W face. Traverse a few feet S past the tree to the base of a shallow gully. Ascend the gully and its left face until it narrows into a chimney. Climb the chimney, and traverse left to a heather patch. Ascend cracks and ribs to the summit. The lack of belay points make pitons advisable. Time: 3 hours from Flapjack Lakes.

THE NEEDLE   ca. 5800

A sharp spire located at Needle Pass.

ROUTE. I, 3. Climb with a single 130-ft. lead to the summit.

MT. CRUISER   6104

A tower-like summit near the north end of Sawtooth Ridge; it is the highest point on the ridge.

First ascent 1937 by P. Crews, D. Dooley, E. Johnson, and R. Layden. The peak is named for the Bremerton Ski Cruisers.

ROUTE 1 (SOUTH CORNER). I, 4. From Flapjack Lakes, take the 1½-mile trail toward Gladys Divide. Just before reaching the Divide, turn right and ascend the 700-ft. chute to a notch in the ridge crest (Needle Pass). Take crampons, as this chute is steep and usually icy. Traverse E on the left side of the pass for 50 ft., then turn to the N and ascend to the ridge crest. Follow on the W side of the ridge northeasterly for ⅛ mile, then cross to the E side and descend a gully just before reaching Mt. Cruiser. Traverse NE on rocky ledges to a small chimney with a cannon hole at its top. Climb through the cannon hole, or over the top, to a platform. Traverse E across the platform ca. 75 ft. and, from a ledge, ascend directly up the face to the ridge crest with a good belay spot. There is a ¼-inch bolt about halfway

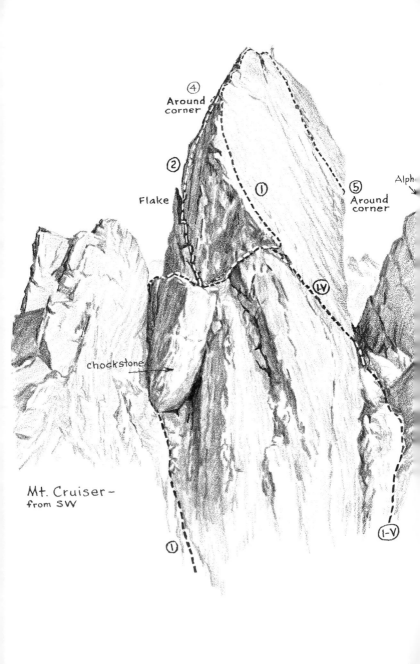

④
Around
corner

②

Flake

⑤
Around
corner

Alph

①

IV

chockstone

Mt. Cruiser —
from SW

①

I-V

up and slightly to the left of this 70-ft. lead. Follow the ridge to the summit. A long rope is needed for the rappel. Time: 3½ hours from Flapjack Lakes.

ROUTE 1-V. I, 5.4. First ascent 1941 by L. Anderson, F. Beckey, and H. Beckey.

Instead of traversing on the rocky ledges of Route 1, continue down the gully to the scree slope. Contour N along the base of the peak and then ascend a short, broad chimney. Next, stem the vertical crack on the E face and traverse left on a narrow ledge. A crack in the overhang provides good piton placement. One move gains a ledge leading to the platform of Route 1.

ROUTE 2 (WEST-SOUTHWEST CORNER). I, 5.7. First ascent 1957 by D. N. Anderson, J. Koch, and J. Richardson.

From the SW platform of Route 1, climb the flake on Mt. Cruiser's W face. From the lower (S) end of the flake, climb directly upward to the ridge crest. Two bolts are in place for protection on this difficult pitch.

ROUTE 3 (NORTHEAST FACE). II, 5.6. First ascent 1958 by D. N. Anderson, R. Hebble, and J. Richardson.

From Gladys Divide, go up and slightly left to a steep crack and gully system in the wall below Mt. Cruiser. Cross the moat and ascend moderate rock for several leads. Higher up, the angle eases off for an exposed scramble to the ridge top. Traverse SW along the crest, and then through a tunnel to a platform at the base of a gendarme on the NE face. From the platform, lead up and slightly left to the ENE corner, following that to a belay spot just below the summit. A 150-ft. rope is necessary for this difficult lead. Time: 6 hours from Flapjack Lakes.

ROUTE 4 (WEST FACE). II, 5.5. First ascent 1959 by D. N. Anderson and R. Harniss.

Climb up immediately to the N (left) of the Needle Pass snow gully of Route 1, until it is possible to scramble up and left (N) to tree-studded ledges. Next, climb a short, mossy gully to the first flake. Move up behind the flake, and drop ca. 20 ft. on the N side to a shallow, open chimney. Ascend the chimney to a good belay stance behind a second flake (from here, a short scramble up and to the right leads to the platform of Route 1). Climb left (N) behind the flake until a large crack pierces the overhang above. Ascend this crack to the top of a third flake. From near this flake's N end, a long lead gains the ridge very close to the summit. Pitons were placed on three pitches. Time: 6 hours from Flapjack Lakes.

ROUTE 5 (EAST FACE). II, 5.7. First ascent 1959 by D. N. Anderson and J. Koch.
Climb onto this triangular wall in its center, and make a left ascending traverse for 20 ft. Next, climb directly over very difficult rock to a small stance. Continue directly up, crossing a side of the triangle on the SE face which leads to the top. Time: 6 hours from Flapjack Lakes.

ROUTE 6 (SOUTHEAST FACE). II, 5.5. First ascent 1967 by D. Benedict and P. Karkiainen.
Climb from the lowest point of the SE face directly to a point about 20 ft. left of the summit. This route is to the right of Route 1 and includes a 140-ft. lead to a 6-inch standing-belay ledge. Piton cracks are scarce.

ALPHA   ca. 6100
Located directly northeast of Mt. Cruiser.
First ascent 1956 by R. Harniss, C. Mecklenburg, and J. Newman.
The approach is made by continuing north past the east face of Mt. Cruiser (see Route 1-V, Mt. Cruiser) or continuing north from Gladys Divide to the Alpha-Cruiser col.

ROUTE 1. I, 2. Ascend a gully on the SE face to the summit.

ROUTE 2. I, 2. Ascend the ridge from the Alpha-Cruiser col.

ROUTE 3 (WEST FACE). I, 5.5. First ascent by J. Duenwald and J. Koch.
Start from a ledge 200 yards N of the route to the Alpha-Cruiser col, and continue up a series of ledges and open chimneys to a prominent tree-covered ledge in mid-face. A short chimney, followed by an exceedingly long, high-angle pitch, and then several easier pitches, gains the summit. Good piton cracks are scarce. Time: 4½ hours from Gladys Divide.

NOODLE NEEDLE   ca. 5600
Located below and on the west side of the ridge top opposite the basin north of Alpha.

First ascent 1957 by D. N. Anderson, J. Koch, and J. Richardson.

ROUTE. I, 5.4, A1. From Gladys Divide, drop slightly and contour into a short gully leading to the basin N of Alpha. The route is on the E side where Noodle Needle connects with the adjoining *Fag Crag*. Ascend an angling crack requiring several pitons before reaching a bolt in place which protects the rest of the short climb.

MT. GLADYS   5600

Located immediately northwest of Gladys Divide.

ROUTE. I, 1. Ascend heather slopes from either Gladys Divide or Black and White Lakes.

MT. HOPPER   6114

Located between the Skokomish and Duckabush Rivers 1 mile southeast of First Divide (4688 ft.).

ROUTE. I, 2. From First Divide, a faint trail contours the S slope to the pass (5010 ft.) ½ mile S of Mt. Hopper. Follow this trail ca. 1 mile, and then ascend directly to the top over easy heather and talus slopes.

An alternate route is a pleasant climb directly up the valley from Home Sweet Home Shelter.

MT. STEEL   ca. 6200

A rocky peak located ca. 1¼ miles west-northwest of First Divide.

ROUTE 1. I, 1. From First Divide, follow meadows to the E face and ascend this face to the summit. Time: 3 hours from First Divide.

ROUTE 2. I, 1. Leave the Marmot Lake trail where it leaves the river ca. 3 miles above Duckabush Camp. The route follows a creek into a little amphitheater on the W side of the summit, where easy slopes lead to the top.

Mt. Duckabush *from* NW

Behind ridge

Behind ridge

② ③ ① i-v

Trail

Hart Lake

D.Molenaar '70

MT. DUCKABUSH   ca. 6250

Located at the head of Nine Stream, Upper O'Neil Creek, O'Neil Creek, and the Duckabush River; the rocky southwest peak is the summit. The 6233-foot northeast peak is identified as Mt. Steel on the 1947 Mt. Steel quadrangle.

ROUTE 1. I, 3. The NW side of the peak is reached by a short drop and ascent from Marmot Lakes. Ascend the eastern (left) of the twin glaciers to its head at the base of the rotten couloir immediately below a prominent notch. Climb the couloir and the E side of the main peak up moderate rock.

The route can be varied by climbing broken rock slopes to the eastern summit from the glacier, then descending heather slopes to the notch, and climbing to the main peak. Time: 4 hours from Marmot Lakes.

ROUTE 2. I, 3. From Marmot Lakes, go to the E side of O'Neil Pass and cross onto the W glacier from the meadows. Ascend to the ridge top and contour through brush on the SW face; cross numerous minor gullies, and continue to gain altitude on moderately difficult rotten rock. After reaching the S ridge, climb directly to the summit.

ROUTE 3. I, 3. First ascent 1937 by N. Bright.

Ascend the steep rock arête between the two glaciers directly to the summit.

Dosewallips Group

The Dosewallips River, with its two main branches, drains a large section of rugged terrain approximately in the middle of the eastern Olympics. Seventeen miles above its mouth in Hood Canal the river branches, the West Fork flowing from Anderson Pass and the main fork from Hayden Pass. Between the two streams is the Anderson Massif with its large glaciers and rugged cliffs. Peaks on the Duckabush-Dosewallips divide, and those adjacent to Hayden Pass, are of gentler contour and lack glaciers. With the exception of the Anderson Massif (7365 ft.), the general peak elevation averages about 6600 ft.

Approaches

1. Dosewallips River: This is the primary approach for all peaks of this group. It is also used for the S side routes of Mt. Constance, Inner Constance, Mt. Deception, and Mt. Mystery (see Constance-Gray Wolf Group, page 83).

The Dosewallips River road leaves U.S. 101 ½ mile N of the river near Brinnon on Hood Canal and extends 15.5 miles to Muscott Flat (1540 ft.). Large trailers are not permitted beyond Elkhorn Campground (11.2 miles). The Dosewallips River trail continues 15.4 miles to Hayden Pass (5847 ft.), with shelters at Dose Forks (1.5 miles, 1736 ft.), Bear Camp (11.0 miles, 3900 ft.), and Dose Meadows (12.8 miles, 4450 ft.). A campsite is at Camp Marion (8 miles, 3350 ft.). The West Fork trail branches from the Dosewallips River trail near Dose Forks, and reaches Anderson Pass (4464 ft.) 10.5 miles from road end. Shelters are located at Diamond Meadow (6.7 miles from road end, 2692 ft.), and just below Anderson Pass (Siberia: 9.8 miles from road

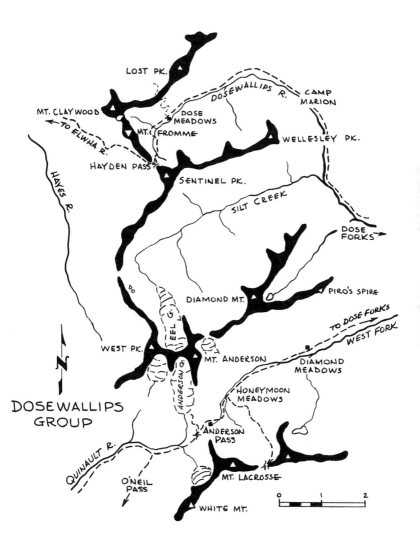

LOST PK.

DOSEWALLIPS R.

CAMP MARION

MT. CLAYWOOD

DOSE MEADOWS

MT. FROMME

WELLESLEY PK.

TO ELWHA R.

HAYDEN PASS

SENTINEL PK.

HAYES R.

SILT CREEK

DOSE FORKS

DO

DIAMOND MT.

PIRO'S SPIRE

EEL G.

TO DOSE FORKS

WEST FORK

WEST PK.

ANDERSON G.

MT. ANDERSON

DIAMOND MEADOWS

HONEYMOON MEADOWS

N

DOSEWALLIPS GROUP

QUINAULT R.

ANDERSON PASS

O'NEIL PASS

MT. LACROSSE

WHITS MT.

0   1   2

end, 4150 ft.). Campsites are at Big Timber (4.2 miles from road end, ca. 2100 ft.) and Honeymoon Meadows (8.9 miles from road end, 3527 ft.).

2. Quinault River: While this approach is used primarily for access to the southern peaks of the Southwestern Group, page 146, it can also be used to reach the Anderson Massif and adjacent peaks including Mt. La Crosse. See Southwestern Group, page 148, for approach details.

Ranger Stations: Dosewallips (Dosewallips River road), Graves Creek (Quinault River road). Guard Station: Corrigenda (Dosewallips River road).

Campgrounds: U.S. 101: Dosewallips State Park, el. 20 ft. (at Brinnon).
Duckabush River Road: Camp Collins, el. 200 ft. (4 miles W of U.S. 101).
Dosewallips River Road: Steelhead, el. 600 ft. (9.5 miles from U.S. 101); Elkhorn, el. 600 ft. (11 miles); Dosewallips, el. 1540 ft. (15.5 miles).
Quinault River Road: Olallie, el. 200 ft. (1 mile E of U.S. 101); Willaby, el. 200 ft. (2 miles); Falls Creek, el. 200 ft. (2½ miles); Graves Creek, el. 550 ft. (18.5 miles).

Vantage Points: Mt. Jupiter can be reached by a 7-mile trail (no water); Sentinel Peak (near Hayden Pass).

Maps: Olympic National Forest; USGS 30-minute Olympic National Park and Vicinity; *The Olympics in Relief,* published by Richard A. Pargeter and George W. Martin; the following 15-minute USGS quadrangles: Mt. Angeles, The Brothers, Mt. Steel, and Tyler Peak.

PIRO'S SPIRE   6301

The easternmost peak in the string of summits located between the West Fork Dosewallips River and Silt Creek. Named for R. Piro, who was killed in the Italian campaign in 1945.
First ascent 1945 by D. Dooley, E. Johnson, and N. Johnson.

Route 1. I, 3. Ascend the wooded mountainside behind Diamond Meadow, bearing slightly E to the summit block. The ascent of the tower on its W side is somewhat exposed.

Route 2. I, 3. First ascent 1956 by F. Armstead, G. Campbell, W. Jacobsen, and K. Spencer.
Take the West Fork trail to just short of the top of a grade about 2 miles beyond Dose Forks. Turn N up the wooded hillside to the E ridge (ca. 2 hours from the trail). A faint wash may be followed to avoid brush on the lower slopes. Follow the ridge W, and traverse into a prominent basin on the N side when it becomes jagged. From the basin, regain the ridge by climbing a shallow gully on the E end of the main massif (2 westerly gullies blank out). Traverse the S side of the summit to a platform just below the short summit tower, where the route joins Route 1. Time: 8 hours from road.

DIAMOND MOUNTAIN   ca. 6800

A high point located on the northeast side of the Anderson Massif.

Route. I, 2. Climb the long mountainside above Diamond Meadow Shelter (6.7 miles from road end) on the West Fork trail. The ascent involves gully, broken rock, and heather scrambling.

MT. ELK LICK   6517

Located on the Duckabush River-West Fork Dosewallips River divide, 1½ miles east of La Crosse Pass.

Route 1. I, 3. First ascent 1971 by B. Burns, H. Favero, F. King, P. Robisch, and J. Stout.
Leave the Duckabush River trail at an elevation of 2100 ft. approximately 3 miles above Tenmile Shelter. This is about 0.1 mile above the point where large and noisy Crazy Creek joins the opposite side of the river and somewhat before another stream crossing. Camp can be made in the vicinity. Note that Crazy Creek is erroneously labeled One Too Many Creek on the 1947 Brothers quadrangle. Obtain water before leaving the trail. Climb due N up steep timbered hillside keeping to the right of

the stream on the left. Continue climbing N past timber line (ca. 5000 ft.) to about 5500 ft. From this point, ascend a ridge NNW to about 6000 ft. where a very steep snow chute is climbed. Continue up the E shoulder to the summit. Time: 7 hours from Tenmile Shelter.

ROUTE 2. I, 2. Reach the W side of the peak by leaving the West Fork trail at Diamond Meadow (6.7 miles) and following Elk Lick Creek through forest and heavy brush. The climb is long.

MT. LA CROSSE   6417
Located at the head of the West Fork and just west of La Crosse Pass.

ROUTE 1. I, 2. From the shelter ½ mile NE of Anderson Pass, climb S up a basin on talus and snow to the ridge top just SE of the summit at 6000 ft. Climb moderate rock and heather to the summit. Time: 3 hours from shelter.

ROUTE 2. I, 3. Leave the talus and snow in the basin (see Route 1), and ascend a prominent snow gully between the N face and the lower NW summit to a loose rock face on the W side of the summit. Time: 3 hours from shelter.

ROUTE 3. I, 2. From La Crosse Pass (5566 ft.), climb W up the ridge (1 mile) to the SE base of the summit, and proceed as for Route 1. Time: 2 hours from trail.

The ridge can be traversed from Mt. La Crosse to White Mountain.

WHITE MOUNTAIN   ca. 6400
Located on the Duckabush-Quinault River divide.

ROUTE 1. I, 2. From Anderson Pass (4464 ft.), make a traversing ascent S 1½ miles to the edge of the White Glacier. From here, climb easy rocks to the summit. Time: 4 hours from Anderson Pass.

ROUTE 2. I, 3. From Mt. La Crosse, cross the saddle to the lower NW summit of La Crosse and traverse the serrated ridge to White Mountain.

ANDERSON MASSIF   7365

This prominent massif bears several large glaciers, which are the sources of the West Fork of the Dosewallips River, Silt Creek, the Quinault River, and the Hayes River. West Peak is the hydrographic apex of the Olympic Peninsula, with its waters flowing into Hood Canal, the Strait of Juan de Fuca, and the Pacific Ocean. Mt. Anderson was named for General T. M. Anderson, the conqueror of Manila in 1898.

WEST PEAK   7365

First ascent 1930 by E. B. Hamilton.

ROUTE 1. II, 3. From Anderson Pass (4464 ft.), 10.5 miles from the Dosewallips River road, ascend the heather ridge on the N via a way trail to the Anderson Glacier moraine (1 hour). There is a campsite near the moraine, in addition to the Anderson Pass shelter (Siberia). Cross the moraine and follow the right side of the glacier ca. 1 mile to the base of a steep snow finger (ca. 35°). Ascend this finger to Flypaper Pass (6500 ft.) at the head of the glacier. The prominent summit immediately SW of Flypaper Pass, sometimes confused with West Peak, is 7100-ft. *Echo Rock*.

From Flypaper Pass descend onto the Eel Glacier. The bergschrund may be a problem in late summer. Traverse NW, gradually climbing until under the steep, rotten NE ridge. Do not climb the ridge! This common mistake leads to an impasse. Instead, traverse N, descending slightly to an obvious scree ledge leading to the NE shoulder. Climb the shoulder westerly until a notch in the horseshoe-shaped ridge is reached. Cross the ridge and climb on the N side ca. 700 ft. Here the ridge narrows, and the only practical route is along the rotten, exposed knife-edge over several false summits. The westernmost summit is the highest. Time: 7 hours from Anderson Pass.

The approach can also be made from Hayden Pass (see Alpine Traverse Section).

MT. ANDERSON   7321

First ascent 1920 by F. B. Lee and party of 20 from Hayden Pass.

ROUTE 1. I, 3. From Flypaper Pass (see Route 1, West

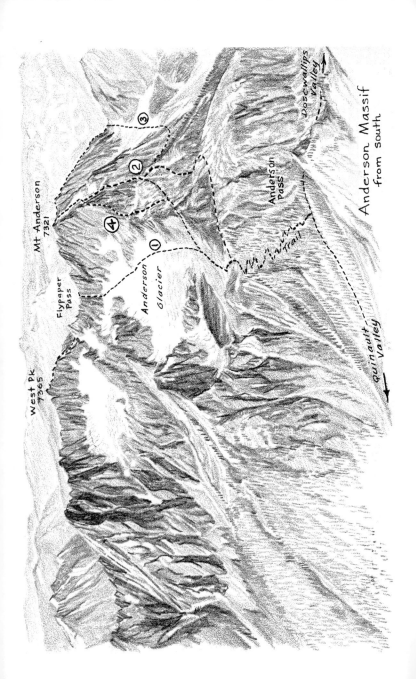

West Pk
7365

Flypaper Pass

Mt Anderson
7321

③

②

④

①

Anderson Glacier

Anderson Pass

Trail

Dosewallips Valley

Quinault Valley

Anderson Massif
from south

Peak), drop 200 ft. onto the Eel Glacier and traverse to the right for a few hundred feet. Climb E up glaciated slopes to a saddle just left of the summit and go S to the summit. Time: 5 hours from Anderson Pass.

The approach can also be made from Hayden Pass (see Alpine Traverse Section).

ROUTE 2. I, 2. From Anderson Pass, take the way trail to its end at the Anderson Glacier moraine. Cross the wooded ridge to the right and contour around on heather and snow about ⅓ mile to a view down a basin with lakes. Descend to the lakes (excellent campsite), then contour past the lakes and climb heather and snow to a col about ½ to ¾ mile beyond the lakes. Above and left of the col, take a steep gully system ca. 800 ft. to scree and snow on the SE side of the peak. From here, climb snow to the summit rocks. The upper part of this route can also be reached using the approach of Route 3. Time: 5 hours from Anderson Pass.

ROUTE 3. I, 2. First ascent 1932 by N. Bright and C. Ullin. From Anderson Pass, take the way trail to Anderson Glacier moraine, and cross the ridge to the NE at the lowest point (ca. ½ mile). Contour NE on alpine meadows and easy snow-covered benches to the ridge NNE of the summit. Ascend WSW to the summit on moderate snow slopes. Time: 5 hours from Anderson Pass.

ROUTE 4. I, 3. First ascent 1930 by E. B. Hamilton and party.

Follow Route 3 to the low point in the ridge (ca. ½ mile) and on 200 to 300 yards to bypass a buttress just N of the notch. Double back W (left) as soon as practical to regain the ridge. Follow this a short distance to the base of a second buttress. Gain the buttress via a steep gully just E (right) of the ridge crest. Follow the crest N to the summit (2 hours from here). Time: 5 hours from Anderson Pass.

References: 1920 *Mountaineer,* 1932 *Trail and Timberline,* 1943 *American Alpine Journal.*

SENTINEL PEAK 6592

Located on the south side of Hayden Pass.

ROUTE. I, 1. From Hayden Pass climb S up an easy talus ridge. Time: 2 hours from Dose Meadows.

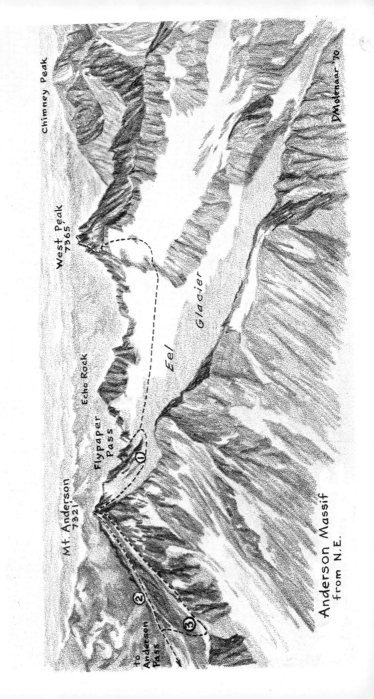

Chimney Peak

West Peak 7365'

Echo Rock

Mt. Anderson 7321

Flypaper Pass

Eel Glacier

①

② ③

to Anderson Pass

Anderson Massif from N.E.

D.Molenaar '70

MT. FROMME (MT. MISCELLANEOUS) 6655

Located north of Hayden Pass. Named for R. L. Fromme, an early Superintendent of Olympic National Forest.

ROUTE 1. I, 1. Climb a gentle talus ridge to the top from 5847-ft. Hayden Pass. Time: 2 hours from Dose Meadows.

ROUTE 2. I, 1. Climb the W ridge from ½ mile NW of Hayden Pass on the Hayes River trail. Time: 2½ hours from Dose Meadows.

MT. CLAYWOOD 6836

Named for Clay Wood, the Adjutant General who ordered Lt. O'Neil on his first Olympic expedition. The USGS names Mt. Claywood as the northerly of two summits northwest of Hayden Pass, though this is in conflict with some references.

ROUTE 1. I, 1. From Mt. Fromme, drop to an ice-bound lake between the 2 summits. A talus shoulder falling to the NE provides an easy final ascent. The lake can be reached directly by climbing steep gully slopes from Dose Meadows. Time: 2 hours from Mt. Fromme.

ROUTE 2. I, 1. From Hayden Pass, follow the Hayes River trail ca. 1 mile to the point where it turns away from the peak down a ridge. Climb northerly up meadow, talus, and easy rock to the summit. Time: 3 hours from Dose Meadows.
Reference: 1920 *Mountaineer*.

LOST PEAK 6515

A prominent though subsidiary peak located north of Dose Meadows.

ROUTE. I, 1. Take the trail N from Dose Meadows to Lost Pass (the 5500-ft. pass just SW of the summit). Ascend easy talus slopes E, swinging around to the E side of the summit near the top. Time: 2 hours from Dose Meadows.

CAMERON PEAK 7192

This is the highest point on the ridge north of Lost Peak.

ROUTE. I, 1. Follow the ridge NE from Lost Peak to the main ridge and contour W to the first summit. Time: 2 hours from Lost Peak.

WELLESLEY PEAK   6758

This pointed peak stands 2 miles northwest of the Silt Creek-Dosewallips River junction.

ROUTE. I, 2. From Dose Meadows, ascend obliquely E through open forests and heather slopes, keeping left of a low buttress, 2½ miles to the NW ridge (about ½ mile from the summit). Some rock scrambling along the ridge leads to the top. Time: 4 hours from Dose Meadows.

MT. JUPITER   5701

The closest high peak to Hood Canal, located between the lower Dosewallips and Duckabush Rivers.

ROUTE. I, 1. Take 7-mile trail (no water) to the summit lookout from the end of the Mt. Jupiter road. This 6⅓-mile road leaves U.S. 101 about ⅓ mile N of the Duckabush River. Time: 7 hours up.

JUPITER CLIFFS

A series of cliffs on the south side of Mt. Jupiter which can be used either as a practice area or as a difficult summit route.

First ascent 1967 by H. Pinsch and G. Tate.

ROUTE. II, 5.5. Park the car at the end of road #2515A (See Duckabush River approach, Skokomish-Duckabush Group, page 39). Walk back down the road ca. 50 yards and turn N up an overgrown logging road which leads to the start of the climb. Start climbing at ca. 1000 ft. just left of a springtime waterfall bed. From this point, the route is via chimneys and ledges and is somewhat restrictive. The climbing eases at ca. 4300 ft. An easier descent can be made by traversing E to avoid the worst of the cliffs. Time: 9 hours to pass the last difficulty.

Reference: 1968 *Mountaineer*.

Constance-Gray Wolf Group

This fine mountain uplift is located in the northeast section of the Olympic Peninsula. It is bordered on the north by the Strait of Juan de Fuca, on the east by Hood Canal, on the south and west by the Dosewallips and Elwha Rivers respectively. The Gray Wolf and Dungeness Rivers on the north side and the Quilcene River on the east side are the remaining large drainage systems. The general peak elevation exceeds that of the mountains to the south, and rivals the Mt. Olympus group to the west. Elongated high barren ridges are typical, with thickly-timbered valleys and a few small lakes near timberline. The highest peaks are located along a horseshoe-shaped ridge enclosing the upper Dungeness River. The Needles, Mt. Deception, and Mt. Mystery are on the west side, while Mt. Constance, Warrior Peak, and the Marmot Pass area lie along the east side.

Collectively, these peaks offer some of the best alpine climbing in the range. A variety of climbing is available, including steep snow and high-angle rock. The only Grade III climbs currently identified in the range are in this group, although numerous climbs are available for the novice as well as the expert. In recent years, as logging roads have been extended up the river valleys, this group has, for the most part, become fairly accessible.

Since this area lies in the Olympic rain shadow, snowfall is the lightest in the range and glaciation is minimal compared with Mt. Olympus and Mt. Anderson to the west. The most important glaciers are the Cameron Glaciers at the head of Cameron Creek; small glaciers on the north sides of Mt. Constance, Mt. Deception, and Mt. Mystery; and Lillian Glacier (little more than a remnant) on McCartney Peak.

83

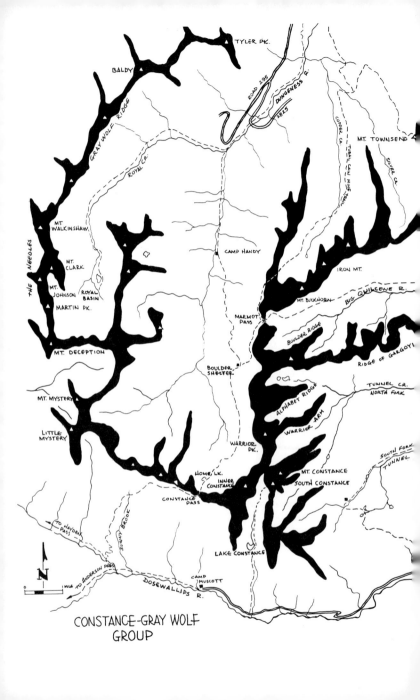

CONSTANCE-GRAY WOLF
GROUP

Approaches

1. Dosewallips River: This approach is used for the S side routes of Mt. Constance, Mt. Deception, and Mt. Mystery. See Dosewallips Group, page 72, for details.

2. Big Quilcene River-Townsend Creek: This approach comprises a complex system of logging roads covering all major tributaries of the Big Quilcene River including both Tunnel Creek and Townsend Creek. It is used primarily for access to the N and E routes on Mt. Constance, the upper Quilcene River peaks, Warrior Arm, and Mt. Townsend. The upper Dungeness River can also be reached via this approach. Since this is a complicated approach, the main access road, including junctions, is described first. Succeeding paragraphs cover the major branch roads.

Leave U.S. 101 1.4 miles S of the town of Quilcene (.4 mile N of the Fish Hatchery). At 1.4 miles, the road branches into Forest Service roads #2812 and #2823. Road #2812, the left branch, is the actual start of the Big Quilcene River-Townsend Creek road. Road #2812 contours 3.2 miles to a junction with the Tunnel Creek road (#2743) and then climbs 6.1 miles to a junction with the upper Big Quilcene road (#272). From this point, #2812 climbs 5.0 miles to Scar Pass (3650 ft.) and then descends into the Little Quilcene River drainage. Between the junction with the upper Big Quilcene road (#272) and Scar Pass, spur roads #2751 and #2764 leave the main road. These lead to the Sink Lake trail and the Mt. Townsend trail respectively. Both trails offer access to Mt. Townsend.

The Tunnel Creek road (#2743) is used to reach the N and E sides of Mt. Constance and as the eastern approach to Warrior Arm. It first crosses the N Fork of Tunnel Creek, then the S Fork, and eventually ends in logged-off areas.

The Tunnel Creek trail starts where road #2743 crosses the S Fork (7 miles from #2812) and climbs ca. 4 miles to the ridge crest separating Tunnel Creek and the Dosewallips River. The trail then descends ca. 3.5 miles to the Dosewallips River road. The Tunnel Creek Shelter is ca. 2.5 miles in from the road.

The upper Big Quilcene River road (#272) provides access to a number of peaks including Mt. Buckhorn, Iron Mountain, Boulder Ridge, and Ridge of Gargoyles. This road, after leaving the main road (#2812), climbs 4.7 miles to the start of the Quilcene River trail, then crosses the river and eventually ends in logged-off areas. The Quilcene River trail climbs 5 miles to Marmot Pass (6000 ft.), and then descends 1.5 miles to the upper Dungeness River trail. Shelters are at the trail head (Tenmile Shelter), and at the junction of the trail descending SW from Marmot Pass and the Dungeness River trail (Boulder Shelter). Established camps are Shelter Rock Camp (2.5 miles, 3600 ft.) and Camp Mystery (4.5 miles, 5400 ft.).

3. Little Quilcene River: This approach is of interest only for access to Mt. Townsend and the Tubal Cain Mine-Dirty Face Ridge area.
The Lords Lake road (Forest Service road #2909) leaves U.S. 101 1.9 miles N of the town of Quilcene. It then climbs 7.0 miles to a junction with road #2812. Road #2812, the left fork, follows the Little Quilcene River, climbing 4.2 miles to Scar Pass.
Note that road #2909 continues past the junction over Bon Jon Pass (2960 ft.) to the Dungeness River, 10.1 miles from the junction. This crossing is much quicker than driving around via U.S. 101.

4. Dungeness River: This approach can be used to reach all the major peaks of this group except Mt. Constance; namely, The Needles, Mt. Deception, Mt. Mystery, and Warrior Peak.
Leave U.S. 101 at Sequim Bay State Park. In ca. 1 mile the road ends at a T junction with the paved county road. Turn left up the county road which becomes Forest Service road #2909 at the Olympic National Forest boundary. At ca. 7.5 miles from U.S. 101, road #295 branches right and descends to the Dungeness River. Road #295 is in actuality the Dungeness River road. After crossing the lower Dungeness River bridge, road #295 climbs 9.8 miles past several numbered spur roads to a junction with road #2825. Road #2825, which branches left, descends 1.6 miles to the upper Dungeness River bridge and the

start of the Dungeness River trail. This road, when complete, will continue 3 more miles into the upper Silver Creek drainage, providing another approach to the Tubal Cain Mine-Dirty Face Ridge area.

The Dungeness River trail follows the river to Royal Creek (1.5 miles) and a junction with the Royal Basin trail (6 miles to Royal Lake). The river trail then gradually climbs to a junction with the Marmot Pass trail (6.0 miles) and continues on past Home Lake (9.4 miles) to Constance Pass (9.8 miles, 5800 ft.). Shelters are Camp Handy (3.2 miles, 3050 ft.) and Boulder Shelter (6.0 miles, 4900 ft.).

Note that the main road (#295) climbs 3.7 miles past its junction with road #2825. The Maynard Burn way trail to the Gray Wolf Ridge can be reached via a cat trail ca. 0.5 mile from the end of this road (3.2 miles from junction with #2825).

5. Northern High Approaches: The Deer Park road leaves U.S. 101 5 miles E of Port Angeles and climbs to the summit of 6007-ft. Blue Mountain. From Deer Park (18.1 miles), the Three Forks trail connects with the Gray Wolf Pass trail, reaching the 6150-ft. pass in 14.5 miles. Shelters are located at Deer Park, Three Forks (4.5 miles, 2100 ft.), Gray Wolf (5 miles, 2000 ft.), and the Falls (10.4 miles, 3900 ft.).

The Hurricane Ridge road leaves U.S. 101 in eastern Port Angeles and climbs 17.8 miles to 5225-ft. Big Meadow. A restaurant, visitor center, and ski facilities are located here. A spur continues 8.4 miles SE to Obstruction Point (6450 ft.). From this point, a trail drops to Grand Lake (3 miles, 4750 ft.) and continues on to Moose Lake (4.1 miles, 5100 ft.). The trail then climbs to Grand Pass (6.0 miles, 6450 ft.) and descends 1.9 miles to the Cameron Creek-Cameron Pass trail to the Dosewallips River.

Ranger Stations: Dosewallips (end of Dosewallips River road), Quilcene (on U.S. 101 just S of Quilcene), Heart O' the Hills (Hurricane Ridge road), and Olympic National Park Headquarters and Museum (Port Angeles). Guard Station: Corrigenda (Dosewallips River road).

Campgrounds: U.S. 101: Seal Rock, el. 50 ft. (2 miles N of Brinnon); Rainbow, el. 800 ft. (5 miles SW of Quilcene); Falls View, el. 450 ft. (4 miles SW of Quilcene); Sequim Bay State Park, el. 100 ft. (4 miles S of Sequim).

Dosewallips River Road: See Dosewallips Group, page 74.

Big Quilcene River-Townsend Creek Road (Forest Service road #2812): Big Quilcene, el. 1700 ft. (4.9 miles from U.S. 101).

Dungeness River Road: Dungeness Forks, el. 1000 ft. (1.0 mile off road #2909, ca. 6.5 miles in on road #2909 from U.S. 101); East Crossing, el. 1050 ft. (on road #295, ca. 10 miles from U.S. 101).

Canyon Creek Road (#2926): Slab Camp, el. 2600 ft. (17 miles SW of Sequim).

Deer Park Road: Deer Park, el. 5400 ft. (18 miles from U.S. 101).

Hurricane Ridge Road: Heart O' the Hills, el. 2000 ft. (5 miles from Port Angeles).

Vantage Points: Deer Park, Hurricane Ridge, Obstruction Point, and Mt. Walker can be reached by road. Mt. Jupiter and Mt. Townsend can be reached by dry trails.

Maps: Olympic National Forest; USGS 30-minute Olympic National Park and Vicinity; *The Olympics in Relief,* published by Richard A. Pargeter and George W. Martin; the following 15-minute USGS quadrangles: Tyler Peak, Mount Angeles.

MT. CONSTANCE   7743

Seen from Seattle, this peak appears as the highest and most massive peak in the Olympic Range. Located northeast of Dose Forks, on the Dosewallips River, it is drained mainly by Tunnel Creek to the east. Here the first ascent was made in 1922 by R. Shellin and A. E. Smith.

The best approach is via the very steep but well-marked Lake Constance way trail which leaves the Dosewallips River road 14.2 miles from U.S. 101. The 2-mile trail climbs 3350 ft. Camp is best located on the E side of Lake Constance at 4650 ft.

ROUTE 1 (MOUNTAINEER ROUTE). II, 3. From Lake Con-

Mt. Constance

Desperation
Peak

Crystal
Pass

Ⅳ ②
①

①

to inner
Constance

Mount Constance (7743')
above Lake Constance (4700'),
eastern Olympics, from south,
showing route to
main massif.

"Trail" from
Dosewallips Rd 2 miles, 3400' elevation gain

D. Molenaar
1970

stance, follow the valley N ca. 1 mile to the last chute leading
E (right) to the main ridge of Mt. Constance (this chute is just
below Crystal Pass). The entrance to this chute is identified by a
house-sized boulder with an overhanging W face. (CAUTION: The
immediately adjacent chute on the S also has a sizable, though
smaller, rock at its entrance). Since the chute is often icy until
early summer, take crampons. Climb E up this steep chute to
the notch at the ridge crest. Go through this notch, turn left,
and then traverse a short distance over ledges on the E side of
the massif to an obvious notch in a minor E-W ridge. Cross
through this notch and descend about 100 ft. to a scree or snow
ledge. Next, contour N ¼ mile across heather or snow slopes,
rock ledges, and two snow gullies, one the "Terrible Traverse."
From here ascend N up one of several short gully systems to

Inner Constance

Mount Constance
from east

DM

open slopes just SE of the summit. Continue to the 60-ft. summit block which is climbed on the N side.

The *Needle* adjoining the summit on the S was first reached by Tyrolean traverse in 1956 by D. N. Anderson and R. Knight.

Time: 7 hours up from Lake Constance, 4 hours down under good conditions.

ROUTE 1-V (COLLEGE ROUTE). II, 3. From the top of the chute (see Route 1), proceed through the notch, turn left, and traverse over ledges on the E side of the massif to an obvious notch in a minor E-W ridge. Cross through this notch, descend several feet and then scramble up westerly, bypassing a minor buttress on the left. Contour slightly upward and N around a depression in the E face below the main ridge to the S side of a second buttress. Continue to the right of this buttress, dropping

Route ① Toward summit of **Constance** from S.E.

slightly to the E side where a narrow sloping ledge (the "Finger Traverse") permits passage. Continue northerly either over another minor buttress to the main ridge or descend a narrow gully onto a permanent snowfield which should be crossed. From here, climb any one of several rock gullies or chimneys to the ridge crest and follow it to the summit block. Time: 7 hours up from Lake Constance, 4 hours down under good conditions.

ROUTE 2 (WEST ARÊTE). III, 5.4. First ascent 1957 by D. N. Anderson, R. Knight, and J. Richardson.
From camp at the head of the Constance valley, climb N to the pass with the small pinnacle in it (Crystal Pass). From behind the small pinnacle, climb the right-hand buttress to the arête and continue near its crest. At the large wall that cuts the arête ⅔ of the way up, traverse up and right on a narrow, rotten ledge for 20 ft. and then climb straight up to a wide tilted ledge leading to a chimney. The arête joins the main ridge ¼ mile S of the summit, which may be reached by traversing the ridge crest on the E side. Time: 10 hours up from Crystal Pass; descent via Route 1 is advisable.

ROUTE 3 (RED DIKE ROUTE). III, 5.5. First ascent 1959 by D. N. Anderson, R. Hebble, and J. Richardson.
From camp in the upper valley (see Route 2), cross Crystal Pass and descend the glacier past the large bergschrund. Just above the level part of the glacier a red dike leads up the wall. Slightly-broken rock on the right of this dike permits upward advance. A long initial lead, with one difficult pitch ca. 80 ft. up, leads to a spot where an anchor protects the next advance over slightly easier rock. From this point, scramble up and right to the highest point on the slabby ledge. Next, climb to the left and up a short pitch of red loose-appearing rock to another ledge. Above, on the left, climb another band of very difficult, unstable-looking red rock, with a traverse into a narrow chimney. Above the chimney, scramble up along the red dike to a point just 200 ft. short of the W ridge. Climb back left and up, making several zig-zags to avoid major difficulties. Go around the corner on a grassy ledge to the final part of the W arête which can be ascended to its junction with the summit ridge and Route 1. Time: 11 hours up; descent via Route 1 is recommended.

ROUTE 4 (EAST FACE). II, 3. This route generally follows the first ascent route.

Leave the Tunnel Creek logging road (#2743) where it crosses the S Fork of Tunnel Creek (7 miles in from main road #2812). Follow the trail 2½ miles to the Tunnel Creek Shelter. A short distance above the shelter, the trail leaves the creek. Leave the trail at this point and climb to the head of the creek. Next, climb NW to the crest of the ridge separating the N and S Forks of Tunnel Creek and descend into the upper N Fork drainage where camp can be made directly beneath Mt. Constance's E face. From camp, climb generally W and then NW via snow or scree gullies to a point near the main ridge crest (ca. 7000 ft.) where the route intersects Route 1-V.

Note that this route can also be reached from the Dosewallips River road. Leave the road at the Karnes Mine road (ca. 13 miles from U.S. 101) and climb N to the ridge crest. Traverse NW to the base of the E face. Time: 6 hours from camp.

ROUTE 5 (NORTHEAST RIDGE). III, 3. First ascent 1958 by K. Heathershaw, R. McKee, R. Oram, and K. Spencer.

Leave the Tunnel Creek road (#2743) where it crosses the S Fork of Tunnel Creek (7 miles from main road #2812). Follow the trail ca. 1½ miles to the 6-mile post. Leave the trail and climb straight up the slope NW to the 5000-ft. pass in the ridge dividing the N and S Forks of Tunnel Creek. Descend into the N Fork of Tunnel Creek where a camping spot can be found at ca. 3900 ft. (about 6 hours from the road). From here proceed westerly ca. ¼ mile to a fairly large level meadow. Ascend the meadow SW through brush to its head. Then climb the right-hand chimney to a large basin (ca. 5000 ft.). Ascend to the head of the basin and traverse to the right until the ridge is reached. Climb along the ridge a short distance until it becomes difficult, then contour SW over very steep slab on the NW face to a shallow gully. Ascend the gully to just below a prominent spire on the ridge crest. The summit can be attained in 1 hour by climbing along the ridge crest, bypassing the gendarmes on either side. The ascent is long, and involves careful routefinding. Time: 9 hours up from camp, 6 hours down (a descent via Route 1 is recommended).

SOUTH SUMMIT   ca. 7600

Located immediately N of the notch at the head of the Constance chute.

First ascent 1958 by T. Hovey and D. Keller.

ROUTE. II, 3. Follow Mt. Constance Route 1-V to the depression in the E face below the main ridge. Climb upward and westerly until the S side of the peak is reached. Climb the obvious chimney to a wide ledge and then traverse left into a second gully to a large rock slab forming a tunnel. Go through the tunnel. A short rock pitch then leads to the flat summit.

References: 1922, 1926, and 1959 *Mountaineer;* 1943 *American Alpine Journal.*

INNER CONSTANCE   ca. 7670

A high massive peak located directly west of Mt. Constance.

First ascent 1939 by D. Harrah and party.

ROUTE 1. II, 4. From Lake Constance (see Mt. Constance), continue N up the valley ca. ¾ mile, until just S of a prominent rock thumb on the left-hand skyline. From this point climb W ascending one of several shallow gullies for about 750 ft. until reaching a prominent snow basin. Continue W crossing the basin, and then climb a broad steep snow chute to the ridge crest. The chute is sometimes icy, and crampons may be needed. Cross to the W side of the ridge, turn right (N) and skirt a false peak, then follow the E side of the ragged ridge N. The summit block is located on the N end of the massif. The top is attained by climbing 100 ft. of steep rotten rock from the S side. If desired, this final pitch may be avoided by following a ledge system around to the right (E) where the final pitch of Route 2 is joined. Time: 5 hours from Lake Constance.

ROUTE 1-V. II, 4. The snow basin may also be reached by continuing up the Constance valley until N of the rock thumb mentioned in Route 1. Turn left and climb SW up snow or scree and easy rock to the basin. From here, follow Route 1 to the summit. Time: 5 hours up from Lake Constance.

ROUTE 2. II, 3. Leave the Constance valley at the same place as in Route 1-V. Climb W directly to what appears to be a ledge rising to the N. This is actually a steep rock-filled chute.

Climb the ridge immediately right of the chute to a headwall, then switchback to the S on a broad ledge around a buttress. From this point, climb N up a short chute reaching a small meadow. Turn SW and climb a ridge to the easy summit block. Time: 4 hours from Lake Constance.

Route 3 (North Buttress). II, 4. First ascent 1957 by R. Harniss and J. Newman.

From the cirque between Inner Constance and Warrior Peak (see Warrior Peak for approach) ascend the right hand buttress SSW up steep rock and snow to the ridge, which leads to the summit. Time: 7 hours from Home Lake or Boulder Shelter.

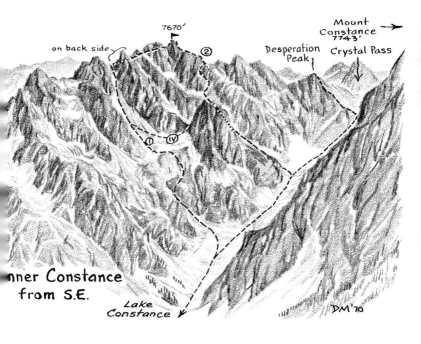

Inner Constance
from S.E.

Lake
Constance

7670'

on back side

Mount
Constance
7743'

Desperation
Peak

Crystal Pass

DM '70

ROUTE 4 (WEST FACE). II, 4. From Home Lake, follow the trail NE a short distance until it climbs into talus slopes falling from the W face. Climb to the head of these talus slopes, then climb generally E via steep gullies and ledges to the main ridge where the route intersects Route 1.

ROTTENROCKEL SPITZ   ca. 6500

The easternmost of 3 pinnacles on a spur ridge extending north-west from the north ridge of Inner Constance (see Route 3 for approach). The pinnacle is identified by a huge cleft completely bisecting it.
First ascent 1962 by B. Gordon, J. Lindsay, and P. Schoening.

ROUTE. I, 4. From the N ridge of Inner Constance, traverse the spur ridge NW for several hundred yards to the base of the pinnacle. A chimney stem then leads to the E ridge which is climbed to the top.

DESPERATION PEAK   ca. 7150

A subsidiary peak located at the north end of the Constance valley.
First ascent 1952 by N. Jacques, L. Nothwang, and R. Strong.

ROUTE. II, 3. From Lake Constance, ascend N up the valley to Crystal Pass. Climb W over broken rock to the jagged SE ridge, and follow the ridge to the false summit. Descend 30 ft. on the W side and cross the col between the false and true summit. Traverse to the N side of the summit face and ascend 40 ft. to the top. Time: 4 hours from Lake Constance.

WARRIOR PEAK   7300

A rocky double-summited peak located ½ mile north of Inner Constance on the Tunnel Creek-Dungeness River divide.
First ascent of both summits 1945 by F. Beckey.

SOUTHEAST SUMMIT   7300

ROUTE. I, 3. Leave the Dungeness River trail ca. 2 miles S of Boulder Shelter (ca. 1½ miles N of Home Lake) near where the creek flows out of the Warrior Peak-Inner Constance cirque.

The Twin Peaks of Warrior from Inner Constance (George W. Martin)

Climb E alongside the creek to reach the mouth of the cirque. From here, Warrior Peak is due N; it is the peak bisected by a prominent couloir. Climb this couloir via snow or steep talus to the saddle between the two summits. Note that several less-prominent easterly gullies, which could be confused with the proper one in bad weather, end in impasses. From the saddle, ascend steep snow on the NW side of the SE peak. The first rock pitch above the snow is difficult. Above this pitch, angle left into a shallow chimney to climb past the last difficulties. From here, a 10-minute scramble leads to the summit. Time: 5 hours from Boulder Shelter.

NORTHWEST SUMMIT   ca. 7285

ROUTE 1. I, 3. For approach, see SE Summit. From the saddle between Warrior's two peaks, climb NW past a pile of spear-like broken rock to the cliff base. Climb the steep shallow gully slightly right (N) of this point to its head (ca. 80 ft.). Contour N on ledges to a scree cone at the base of a second gully. Climb an easy gully to the ridge, which then leads to the summit. Time: 5 hours from Boulder Shelter.

ROUTE 2. I, 3. First ascent 1968 by A. Bloomer, G. Kelsey, R. Latz, H. Pinsch, and K. Spencer.
The route starts at the Warrior Peak-Alphabet Ridge saddle. Early in the season the best approach to this saddle is via the Dungeness River trail; leave the trail ca. 1¼ miles S of Boulder Shelter (at the Park boundary) and climb snow and scree gullies to the 6700-ft. saddle. Later in the year when the snow is gone, the easiest approach is to follow the Charlia Lakes way trail to the Boulder Ridge-Alphabet Ridge saddle. The Charlia Lakes trail leaves the Dungeness River trail just S of Boulder Shelter. From the end of the trail at the saddle, climb over Cloudy Peak and descend several hundred feet over easy snow or scree to the Warrior Peak-Alphabet Ridge saddle. Climb the broad ridge S from the saddle. After a short distance the route leaves the ridge crest, contouring onto the W side via ledges and talus. Follow the line of least difficulty past a number of steep chimneys. The ledges end abruptly behind a small pinnacle on the SW corner of the peak. Climb the only avenue of ascent, a short gully followed by easy rock and scree. The next obstacle, a

Constance, Inner Constance and Warrior from Ridge of Gargoyles
(Keith Spencer)

near vertical pitch, is climbed on its right-hand side; the rock is loose. Above this pitch, proceed through an obvious crack in the ridge. Climb to the summit avoiding the airy ridge crest in favor of an easy scramble on the N side of the ridge. Time: 6 hours up from Boulder Shelter; the easiest descent is via Route 1.

ROUTE 3. I, 3. First ascent 1960 by D. N. Anderson, D. Devin, S. Johnson, and J. Munson.
From the Warrior Peak-Alphabet Ridge saddle (see Route 2 for approach), climb the broad ridge S for several hundred yards to the base of one of several prominent chimneys. Climb one of these chimneys to gain the upper slopes of the peak and then continue S over snow and broken rock to the small summit. Time: 6 hours up from Boulder Shelter; 3 hours down via Route 1.

WARRIOR ARM   ca. 6900

A major ridge running east from Warrior Peak. This seldom-visited though interesting area offers numerous climbs of varying difficulty on fairly good rock.

There is no easy access to this ridge. The east end (e.g., The Squaw and The Papoose) can best be reached from a camp in the North Fork of Tunnel Creek (see camp and approach for Mt. Constance Route 5). The west portion (i.e., The Brave and Tower 6700) is most easily reached from Boulder Shelter on the Dungeness River.

Only the major summits are covered; they are listed in order from west to east. There are several lesser summits between Tower 6700 and The Squaw.

Reference: 1969 *Mountaineer*.

THE BRAVE   ca. 6900

First ascent 1968 by A. Bloomer, G. Kelsey, R. Latz, and K. Spencer.

ROUTE. II, 4. After camp at Boulder Shelter, take the Charlia Lakes way trail to the Boulder Ridge-Alphabet Ridge saddle. Climb S to the summit rocks of Cloudy Peak and then descend S over talus or easy snow to the Warrior Peak-Alphabet Ridge saddle. From here, descend the eastern basin ca. 750 ft. until a moraine on the S side of the valley is reached. Ascend the moraine to reach the lower terminus of a hidden snow basin which descends from the Warrior Peak-Brave col. Climb to this col. From the col, ascend easterly over snow, snow and rock mixed, and a short rock pitch to a sloping ledge. Contour left to the base of a hidden chimney. This chimney, the climb's chief difficulty, requires one long lead to surmount. From here, follow a ledge on the N side beneath the ridge crest to a second chimney. Continue past this chimney a few feet and then climb a short exposed pitch past the final difficulties. A short scramble leads to the tiny summit. Time: 8 hours from Boulder Shelter, 4 hours down.

The Brave's somewhat lower E Tower can be reached by descending from the main summit. The ascent appears fairly difficult. Also, it should be possible to climb the E Peak from The Brave-Tower 6700 col via several hundred feet of very steep slab.

TOWER 6700   ca. 6700

ROUTE. For approach, see route for The Brave. Ascend the moraine to reach the hidden snow basin. Cross this basin to an obvious couloir (crampons are recommended; also, the bergschrund becomes difficult to cross late in the summer). Ascend this steep couloir to The Brave-Tower 6700 notch. The final 200 ft. are difficult.

THE SQUAW   ca. 6300

First ascent 1967 by A. Bloomer, G. Kelsey, R. Oram, H. Pinsch, and K. Spencer.

ROUTE. II, 2. From the camp described in Mt. Constance Route 5, proceed NW through a meadow to the creek flowing from the glacier on the N side of Mt. Constance. Cross the creek and climb N through timber a short distance, then bear NE to an old burn. Ascend the burn and then climb through a prominent break in the lower cliffs. Next, ascend westerly keeping well under the summit of The Papoose to just below The Squaw-Papoose col. An easy scramble leads to the summit. Time: 4 hours from camp.

The Squaw-Papoose col could also be reached via a snow chute on the N side after an approach as described for The Brave. Such an approach would be longer.

THE PAPOOSE   ca. 6100

The easternmost summit on Warrior Arm.

ROUTE. II, 2. See route description for The Squaw. From The Squaw-Papoose col, climb easterly along the broken ridge to the summit. Time: 4 hours from camp.

ALPHABET RIDGE   ca. 7000

An east-west ridge, consisting of a number of summits and rock spires, bordered by Charlia Lakes on the north and Warrior Peak on the south. The major summits are presented from west to east.

The approach begins at Boulder Shelter on the Dungeness River trail. Proceed S along the trail for several hundred yards to the unmarked Charlia Lakes way trail. Ascend the trail to the broad saddle overlooking Charlia Lakes.

Reference: 1969 *Mountaineer*.

CLOUDY PEAK   ca. 7000

The rounded summit immediately above and south of the saddle.

ROUTE. I, 2. Climb S to the summit up steep snow or scree. Time: 3 hours from Boulder Shelter.

ZEE SPIRE   ca. 6950

First ascent 1958 by A. Bloomer, R. Oram, and K. Spencer.

ROUTE. I, 3. Traverse the ridge E from Cloudy Peak and climb Zee Spire via the W side.

WHY SPIRE   ca. 6900

First ascent 1958 by A. Bloomer, R. Oram, and K. Spencer.

ROUTE. I, 3. Continue E from Zee Spire to the summit.

EX-SPIRE   ca. 6950

First ascent 1958 by A. Bloomer, R. Oram, and K. Spencer.

ROUTE. I, 4. Approach from Why Spire. Traverse under the S side and climb the E corner. The shallow 120-ft. chimney on the S side has also been climbed.

CURIOSITY PEAK   ca. 7000

First ascent 1958 by A. Bloomer, R. Oram, and K. Spencer.

ROUTE. I, 3. Continue E from Ex-Spire over broken rock to the summit. Time: 4 hours from Boulder Shelter.

ETCETERA SPIRE   ca. 6900

First ascent 1968 by A. Bloomer, G. Kelsey, R. Latz, and H. Pinsch.

ROUTE. I, 3. From Curiosity Peak, follow the narrowing ridge NE for ca. 300 yards. Climb the E side.

INFINITY TOWER   ca. 6900

First ascent 1968 by D. Muntz and R. Olson, Jr.

ROUTE. II, 3, A1. From Curiosity Peak, follow the narrowing ridge NE to Etcetera Spire. Traverse along the N side of Etcetera Spire and then follow the narrow broken ridge ca. 300 yards to the Tower's base. The 150-ft. Tower is vertical on all sides. The first ascent party threw a codline over the top and accomplished a prusik ascent. Time: 8 hours from Boulder Shelter.

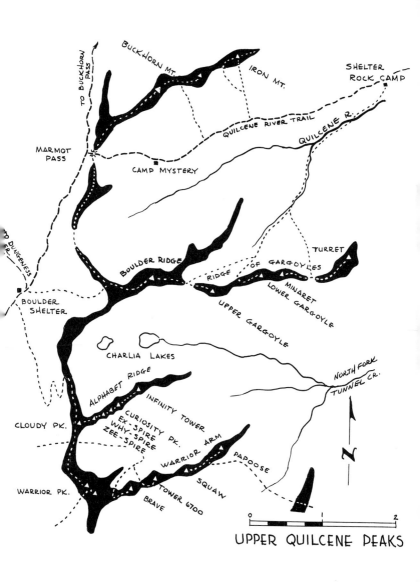

UPPER QUILCENE PEAKS

BOULDER RIDGE   6852

Located 1 mile south-southeast of Marmot Pass above the head-waters of the Quilcene River.

ROUTE 1. I, 3. Leave the Quilcene River trail at Marmot Pass and climb S over heather and scree for about ¾ mile to the base of Boulder Ridge, which runs E from this point. Bear left (E) over talus and easy rock; remain fairly low on the N side of the ridge to avoid as much of the time-consuming jagged ridge as possible. Climb to the ridge crest when the N slope starts to become cliffy. Climb E along the broken ridge to the summit. Time: 4 hours from Marmot Pass.

ROUTE 2 (SOUTHEAST SHOULDER). I, 2. First ascent 1968 by R. Etten, K. Heathershaw, and K. Spencer.
For approach, see the Upper Gargoyle route description. From the Upper Gargoyle-Boulder Ridge saddle, climb WNW over scree and broken rock to the easy summit. Time: 7 hours from Quilcene River road.

RIDGE OF GARGOYLES   ca. 6400

A string of sharp rock summits lying immediately southeast of Boulder Ridge forming the south wall of the upper Quilcene River. These summits are described in order from west to east.
Reference: 1969 *Mountaineer*, 1969 *American Alpine Journal*.

UPPER GARGOYLE   ca. 6400

First ascent 1968 by R. Etten, K. Heathershaw, and K. Spencer.

ROUTE. II, 3. Leave the Quilcene River trail at Shelter Rock Camp (ca. 2½ miles from the road). Follow the N riverbank for about ⅔ mile and then cross the stream to a rockslide. Traverse the rockslide W for several hundred yards and then contour into timber and back to the river (S Fork). Follow the S Fork to just below a water cascade formed by a side creek (several campsites can be found in this general area). Continue climbing along the main stream; the going here is steep and brushy. The easiest passage is high, just below the cliffs on the S side of the canyon. Above the cliff band the gradient lessens. Continue along near the creek, generally following the easiest path. Note that this creek flows from the S side of Boulder Ridge; therefore be alert to traverse SW into the scree and snow basin separating Boulder Ridge and the Ridge of Gargoyles. Climb to near the Upper Gargoyle-Boulder Ridge saddle; then climb a prominent snow-and-rock couloir on the NW corner of Upper Gargoyle. About ⅔ of the way up this couloir bear left over broken rock to a gully system. Climb this system and the steep rock pitch immediately above it. Some scrambling and several short rock pitches lead to the summit. Time: 8 hours from the road.

LOWER GARGOYLE   ca. 6150

ROUTE. II, 3. Use the approach for Upper Gargoyle until the lower end of the aforementioned snow-and-scree basin is reached. Bear left (S) and climb to the Upper Gargoyle-Lower Gargoyle col via steep snow or scree. A short steep rock climb leads to the summit. Time: 7 hours from road.

MINARET   ca. 6200

ROUTE. I, 4. This route starts at the water cascade mentioned in the Upper Gargoyle route description. Climb the right side of the water cascade to avoid brush, and then bear left to miss the lower cliff band. Above the cliffs, continue generally S over brush, boulders, scree, and snow to the Turret-Minaret col. From here, climb W over slabs and buttresses to the 100-ft. summit tower which can be climbed on the E side. Time: 7 hours from road.

TURRET   ca. 6350

First ascent 1967 by R. Etten, K. Heathershaw, and K. Spencer.

ROUTE. I, 3. For route to Turret-Minaret col see Minaret. From the col, climb the ridge E. The false summit can be bypassed on the N side via slabs. A short scramble then leads to the summit. Time: 7 hours from road.

MT. BUCKHORN   6988

A double-summited peak ca. 1 mile northeast of Marmot Pass. So named because the twin peaks resemble deer horns. The Southwest Peak is higher, but the Northeast Peak is a much more challenging climb.

SOUTHWEST PEAK   6988
ROUTE. I, 1. From Marmot Pass, climb NE over heather and scree to the summit. Time: 1 hour from Marmot Pass.

NORTHEAST PEAK   6956
ROUTE. I, 3. Leave the Quilcene River trail about ½ mile E of Camp Mystery and climb snow or steep talus to the col between Buckhorn's two peaks. From here, climb the steep exposed ridge NE to the summit. The NE Peak can also be reached by descending from the SW Peak. Time: 3 hours from trail.

IRON MOUNTAIN   ca. 6950
A multi-summited rock peak located ½ mile northeast of the Northeast Peak of Mt. Buckhorn.

ROUTE. I, 3. Leave the Quilcene River trail about 1 mile above Shelter Rock Camp where the trail completely leaves the trees. Climb up scree or snow and then up a major gully system to the notch between and just below the main peaks. The SW summit is the highest. Time: 6 hours from the Quilcene River road.

MT. WORTHINGTON (COPPER PEAK)   ca. 6900
Located ¾ mile northeast of Iron Mountain and ¾ mile east of Buckhorn Lake.

ROUTE. I, 3. Leave the Quilcene River trail at Shelter Rock Camp (ca. 2½ miles from road) and climb due N to the 6100-ft. saddle in the E-W ridge connecting Mt. Worthington and Hawk Peak. Climb NW to the summit over steep rotten rock. Time: 5 hours from road.

HAWK PEAK   ca. 6550
Located ¾ mile northeast of Mt. Worthington and ½ mile west-southwest of Silver Lake.

ROUTE. I, 2. From the Worthington-Hawk Peak saddle (see Mt. Worthington for approach), follow the ridge E to the easy summit. Time: 4 hours from road.

WELCH PEAKS   ca. 6100

Located 1 mile south of Mt. Townsend.

ROUTE 1. I, 2. Approach via the S side Mt. Townsend trail (see Quilcene River approach). From Camp Windy, follow the new trail to the Welch Peaks-Mt. Townsend saddle. Leave the trail and climb the ridge S to the highest summit. Time: 2 hours from Camp Windy.

ROUTE 2. I, 4. First ascent 1967 by D. Miss and R. Olson, Jr. From Camp Windy, climb SE to Upper Windy Lake through brush via stream beds. Next, climb the large talus fan at the base of the chute leading from the main Welch Peak. About ⅔ of the way up this chute, a chimney on the right with a tree at its base signals the start of serious climbing. Climb the chimney to a large comfortable ledge. Next, climb up a wide chimney for three rope leads to just N of the summit. The rock is friable and there is danger of rockfall. Time: 3 hours from Camp Windy.

MT. TOWNSEND   6280

This northeastern cornerpost of the Olympics is a north-south ridge bordered by Bon Jon Pass on the north, Silver Creek on the west, and Sink Lake on the southeast. It is becoming increasingly popular as a winter and spring climb due to easy access. Route 3 is an excellent ski tour. A trail runs across the summit.

ROUTE 1. I, 1. Early in the season when the Bon Jon Pass road (#2909) is closed by snow, leave the upper Little Quilcene River road (#2812) ca. 2¼ miles above the 2812-2909 junction. A sign indicates "Little Quilcene Trail" which goes to the summit. This trail crosses road #2852 at Last Water Camp (ca. 1 mile). A few hundred yards above here, the trail breaks out onto open slopes (Little River Summit). Most early-spring groups leave the trail and follow the easy ridge to the summit.

Later in the year, continue on road #2909 past its junction with road #2812. Proceed over Bon Jon Pass and ½ mile farther to spur road #2909J. Turn left and follow the spur road a short distance to road #2852. Turn right and follow #2852 ca. 1½ miles to its unmarked crossing of the Little Quilcene trail. Time: 3 hours from road #2852.

ROUTE 2. I, 1. Leave the Big Quilcene River-Townsend Creek road (#2812) ca. 15 miles in from U.S. 101 (1 mile S of Scar Pass). Follow trail ca. 3 miles to S side of peak (open slopes near Camp Windy). From here, follow trail or easy meadows to summit. Time: 4 hours from Sink Lake.

ROUTE 3. I, 1. Use road #2812 approach as in Route 1 early season; however, continue past the Little Quilcene River trail, past a creek and halfway through logged slopes. An unmarked logging road leaves main road here (ca. 1 mile past trail). Turn W to the uppermost section of this road which ends in a hidden logged-off basin. Climb up through heavy timber, following a small creek. At the upper reaches of the creek, diagonal up and right to open slopes and a saddle (ca. 4400 ft.). Drop from saddle and continue across a basin to cliffs and couloirs on the face or climb E ridge direct. Time: 4 hours from road.

MT. MYSTERY   7631

A bulky peak located between Deception Creek and the head of Heather Creek, a tributary of the Dungeness River.

ROUTE 1. I, 3. From 1 mile beyond Dose Forks on the Dosewallips River trail, take the Constance Pass trail to its crossing of Sunny Brook (ca. 5000 ft.). Leave the trail and climb NW to the low point of Del Monte Ridge (W of Point 6666). Traverse the ridge NW ca. 1½ miles to Gunsight Pass (ca. 6350 ft.) between Mystery and Little Mystery on the S. Cross the pass to the W side of Mt. Mystery and climb shale slopes. Contour N (left) ca. ¼ mile at the top of the shale to the summit block. Next, cross the ridge to the E side (right) and climb back left on good rock to the summit. Time: 6 hours from Sunny Brook Meadows on the Constance Pass trail.

Gunsight Pass can also be reached by a complete traverse of Del Monte Ridge from Constance Pass.

ROUTE 2. I, 3. Leave the Dosewallips River trail 50 yards above Deception Creek (ca. 8 miles from road) and climb E paralleling the creek following a faint way trail. Climb to just below the confluence of the two branches of Deception Creek where camp can be made. From camp, climb SE ca. 1½ miles to reach Gunsight Pass and a junction with Route 1.

ROUTE 3. II, 3. From the Deception Creek camp of Route 2, ascend the left fork into lower Deception Basin (beautiful camp spot). Climb right (SSE) up the stagnant glacier to its head. Turn right (W) and ascend rock ridge to the summit block. Time: 5 hours from Deception Basin camp.

LITTLE MYSTERY   6941

Located immediately south of Mt. Mystery.

ROUTE. I, 3. Climb the E side from Gunsight Pass via a steep snow or scree gully to the ridge. Follow the ridge N to the summit. Time: 2 hours from Gunsight Pass.

MT. FRICABA   7134

An elongated double-summited peak located northeast of Mt. Mystery at the head of Deception Basin.

First recorded ascent 1957 by D. Bechlem (Northeast Summit) and J. Newman (Southwest Summit).

ROUTE. I, 2. Climb E from upper Deception Basin. The peak could also be approached from either Royal Basin (see Needles for approach) or Del Monte Ridge. Time: 3 hours from upper Deception Basin.

MT. DECEPTION   7788

The highest peak in the eastern Olympics even though it cannot be seen from Seattle. It is located 1½ miles northwest of Mt. Mystery between Deception Creek and Royal Creek.

ROUTE 1. I, 2. Leave the Dosewallips River trail ca. 8 miles from the road (ca. ½ mile below Camp Marion). Ascend the ridge separating Cub Creek and Deception Creek to alpine meadows. At about 5500 ft. bear diagonally right (NE) off the ridge; a long but easy talus and broken rock slope leads to the summit. Time: 6 hours from the trail.

ROUTE 2. I, 2. From a camp just below the confluence of the two branches of Deception Creek (see Mt. Mystery, Route 2), climb N first through meadows, then up wooded hillside and finally over talus slopes to an eventual intersection with Route 1 at ca. 6000 ft. Time: 4 hours from camp, 6 hours from the trail.

Route 3. I, 2. From Royal Lake (see Needles for approach) climb S then SW to a small lake in upper Royal Basin (camp could be placed here). Make an ascending traverse westerly over talus and easy rock to the low point in the Deception-Martin Peak ridge. Cross to the W side of the ridge and descend S to the glacier. Continue S climbing past a bergschrund and up a steep (40°) but short snow slope to the summit ridge. From here, bear left (E) and climb the easy ridge to the summit. Time: 6 hours from Royal Lake.

Route 4 (Honeymoon Route). I, 3. First ascent 1965 by A. Bloomer and D. Bloomer. The route starts at the low point in the Mt. Deception-Martin Peak ridge (see Route 3). Bear left (E) of the severe ridge crest into a steep (45°) snow gully which climbs S towards the summit. Climb this gully to its exit on the ridge just below the summit. Time: 5 hours from Royal Lake.

Route 5 (Northeast Face). I, 3. First ascent 1962 by K. Hilton, J. Merkel, J. Munson, and J. Parolini.
From Royal Lake (see Needles for approach), climb S then SW to a small lake in upper Royal Basin (camp could be placed here). Climb SW over glacial moraine for nearly 1 mile to the base of a large snow (or mud) slope on the W edge of the NE face. Climb the steep slope to its head, then directly up to the summit. Rockfall is a problem. Time: 5 hours from Royal Lake.

Route 6. I, 2. Climb 3½ miles from the Dosewallips River trail to Gray Wolf Pass (6150 ft.). Traverse E from the Pass in alpine meadows on the S side of the ridge for ca. 3 miles to where Route 1 is joined in alpine meadows. Time: 4 hours from Gray Wolf Pass.

GILHOOLEY TOWER   ca. 7400

A prominent tower located ¼ mile northwest of Mt. Deception. First ascent 1963 by D. N. Anderson, H. Pinsch, and J. Pinsch.

Route. I, 4. Climb from the SW corner. The first lead is the most difficult. Time: 1 hour from base.

SNIFTER SPIRE   ca. 7000

This block-like spire is located on the east flank of Mt. Deception just above the Deception Basin-Royal Basin divide. See Needles for approach.

Mt Mystery

Little Mystery

① ③

②

Mt Deception

⑤ ④

Gilhooley Tower

③

③V

③

Deception Glacier

Martin Peak

al asin

urprise Basin

DM

ts Deception and Mystery
om north

First ascent 1962 by K. Hilton, J. Merkel, J. Munson, and J. Parolini.

ROUTE. I, 5.3, A2. From Royal Lake, climb S then SW to a small lake in Upper Royal Basin. Proceed S over glacial moraine nearly 1 mile to the pass just E of Mt. Deception (Royal Basin-Deception Basin divide). From the pass, climb W to the base of Snifter Spire and then traverse the N side via Class 4 slabs to the W side of the Spire. Climb 40 ft. up the W corner of the block (5.3) and then traverse steep slab right to the overhang which requires aid. Above the overhang, 50 ft. of 5.2 climbing leads to the top. Time: 5 hours from Royal Lake.

THE NEEDLES   ca. 7650

An extensive north-south ridge of rock peaks and pinnacles located between Mt. Deception on the south, the Gray Wolf Ridge on the north, and Royal Basin on the east. This ridge contains the highest collective group of peaks and spires in the Olympic Range, and offers some of the most interesting rock climbing in the range. Only the major peaks and spires are covered in this description, but innumerable short rock climbs of varying difficulty are available throughout the area.

Leave the Dungeness River road (#2825) at the upper Dungeness River bridge (see Dungeness River approach) and follow the river trail ca. 1½ miles to a junction with the Royal Creek trail. Follow the 6-mile Royal Creek trail to Royal Lake (5100 ft.). An excellent camp can be made ¼ mile southwest of the lake under a large overhanging boulder called Shelter Rock.

Petunia Peak on the east side of Royal Basin offers an excellent vantage point for surveying the entire massif. Following are route descriptions for the major climbs in the area, which are covered from south to north.

MARTIN PEAK   ca. 7550

The southernmost peak in The Needles, located 1 mile north of Mt. Deception.

First ascent 1940 by E. Johnson and G. Martin via Route 3.

ROUTE 1. I, 3. From Shelter Rock in Royal Basin, cross the meadow W to the waterfall. Climb the left side of the waterfall

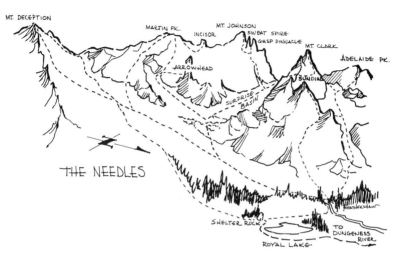

to a broad grassy ledge. Traverse left (S) ca. 20 minutes into a narrow valley. Proceed up the valley to the terminal moraine of Surprise Basin; continue past the terminal moraine climbing towards the ridge separating Martin Peak and Mt. Deception. Several hundred yards past the S edge of the moraine, turn right and climb directly toward the ridge crest. Several rocky gullies offer relatively easy passage to the upper shoulder of Martin Peak. From this point scramble NW to the summit. Time: 4 hours from Royal Lake.

ROUTE 2. I, 4. First ascent 1961 by J. Munson and J. Parolini.

Climb to the top of the terminal moraine of Surprise Basin after an approach via Route 1. Proceed to the SW boundary of the moraine and ascend a chute to just below The Arrowhead, a prominent 120-ft. spire. Next, ascend chimneys to the left (S) of The Arrowhead. Above The Arrowhead it is a scramble to the summit. Time: 4 hours from Royal Lake.

ROUTE 3. I, 3. Follow the ridge N from the low point in the Mt. Deception-Martin Peak ridge (see Mt. Deception Route

3 for approach). The ascent, mostly along ledges below the ridge crest, appears more difficult than it is. Time: 3 hours up from the saddle; descent via Route 1 is recommended.

THE ARROWHEAD   ca. 7000

A 120-ft. rock spire located on the east flank of Martin Peak.
First ascent 1962 by K. Hilton, J. Merkel, J. Munson, and J. Parolini.

ROUTE. I, 5.6. Approach via Route 2, Martin Peak. From the notch between Martin Peak and The Arrowhead, a small ledge leads right (S) to the W edge of the vertical S face. Traverse E (across the face) 30 ft. on small holds, then climb to the summit. Time: 4 hours from Royal Lake.

THE INCISOR   ca. 7350

A prominent rock tooth located 300 yards north of Martin Peak.
First ascent 1958 by K. Heathershaw and R. McKee.

ROUTE. I, 5.4. From the summit of Martin Peak, descend 50 ft. on the E side and then traverse N over snow, ledges, and broken rock below the ridge crest. Next, a short rock climb leads to the SE corner of The Incisor block. From here, make an exposed traverse N, angling up along a slight depression to the low N end of the summit ridge. Straddle the knife ridge to the summit. Descend by rappelling from the N end of the ridge. Expansion bolts are needed for setting up the rappel. Time: 2 hours from Martin Peak.

MT. JOHNSON   ca. 7650

The highest peak in The Needles.
First ascent 1940 by E. Johnson and G. Martin via Route 2.

ROUTE 1. II, 4. From Shelter Rock in Royal Basin, cross the meadow W to the waterfall. Climb the left side of the waterfall to a broad grassy ledge. Traverse left (S) ca. 20 minutes to a narrow valley. Proceed up the valley to the terminal moraine of Surprise Basin. Climb to the top of the moraine and then proceed to within 100 yards of the pass at the head of the basin (2½ hours from Royal Basin). From this point, climb W (left) up scree and snow to a sloping ledge that leads S. Follow this ledge to an easy talus gully and ascend the gully to a small second basin. Climb toward the head of this basin bearing left to bypass Sweat Spire on the S. Continue up gullies to the eastern base of the summit block where a 100-ft. chimney can be stemmed to the summit. Time: 6 hours from Royal Lake.

Route I-V. II, 5.1. First ascent 1958 by K. Heathershaw, R. McKee, F. Spencer, and K. Spencer.

This route is recommended if ascent of either Gasp Pinnacle or Sweat Spire is also planned. From the entrance of the small second basin of Route 1, climb scree and easy rock on the right side of the basin toward the notch between Gasp Pinnacle and Sweat Spire. Two Class 5 rock pitches lead to the platform between Mt. Johnson and the spires. From the platform, climb W for 200 ft. to the summit block of Mt. Johnson, which can be climbed on the E side via the 100-ft. chimney of Route 1. Time: 6 hours from Royal Lake.

Route 2. II, 4. Climb from the S via a traverse of the 1-mile jagged ridge from Martin Peak. Time: 3 hours from Martin Peak.

Route 3. II, 4. First ascent 1946 by J. Vance and party.

Climb through the pass at the head of Surprise Basin (see Route 1) and make a descending traverse to the SW. Climb the gully system directly below the summit to just below the top. Time: 7 hours from Royal Lake.

SWEAT SPIRE   ca. 7580

A 200-ft. rock needle located just east of Mt. Johnson.

First ascent 1962 by K. Hilton, J. Merkel, J. Munson, and J. Parolini.

Route. II, 5.2. From the platform (see Route 1-V, Mt. Johnson), traverse S between the Spire and a large rock flake; next, climb to the top on the rib just left of the gully on the SW side. Time: 6 hours from Royal Lake.

GASP PINNACLE   ca. 7540

Located just north of Sweat Spire.

First ascent 1958 by K. Heathershaw, R. McKee, F. Spencer, and K. Spencer.

Route. II, 4. From the platform (see Route 1-V, Mt. Johnson), cross boulders to the W side of the pinnacle. Here, a 40-ft. climb leads to a narrow ledge which can be traversed N behind a flake to the summit ridge. Climb the exposed ridge to the summit. Time: 6 hours from Royal Lake.

SUNDIAL   ca. 7150

Located ½ mile west of Royal Lake. So named because from Royal Basin the approximate time of morning can be told by watching the sunlight progress down the east face.

First ascent 1944 by A. Degenhardt and W. Degenhardt.

ROUTE 1. I, 3. From Shelter Rock in Royal Basin, cross the meadow W to the waterfall. Climb the left side of the waterfall to a broad grassy ledge. Continue climbing W through a series of minor cliffs to a buttress forming the right boundary of a major scree gully. Contour left around the buttress into the gully and climb to the notch at its head. From the notch, traverse S, gradually climbing across the E face over moderately difficult rock to the final short ascent of the two summit blocks. Time: 3 hours from Royal Lake.

ROUTE 2. I, 3. From Shelter Rock in Royal Basin, cross the meadow W to the waterfall. Climb the left side of the waterfall to a broad grassy ledge. Bear right (N) and traverse just below the cliff band for ca. 20 minutes. Ascend a short gully to a slight notch in a minor E-W ridge. Continue to contour around the cliff band descending slightly into an open meadow. Bear hard left, dropping a short distance into a small snow basin. Ascend the snow finger at its head to a large basin (Belvedere Basin). From this basin, traverse SE over permanent snowfields to the N side of Sundial. Climb a chimney-gully system ca. 300 ft. to the notch mentioned in Route 1. Follow Route 1 to the summit. Time: 4 hours from Royal Lake.

MT. CLARK (BELVEDERE)   7528

This jagged peak, perhaps the best climb in The Needles, is located directly across Surprise Basin from Mt. Johnson. Originally named Belvedere, the peak was recently and officially renamed Mt. Clark in honor of Irving M. Clark, prominent conservationist.

First ascent 1940 by E. Johnson and G. Martin via Route 2.

ROUTE 1. II, 3. First ascent 1958 by C. Broberg, K. Heathershaw, R. McKee, and K. Spencer.

From the pass at the head of Surprise Basin (see Route 1, Mt. Johnson), traverse a sloping ledge which climbs back SE for 100 yards. At this point, climb a broken rock gully past a large boulder. Above this rock, climb the right-hand branch gully to a notch in the SE ridge. Cross the latter and descend to a ledge on the E face. Traverse it northerly 200 yards to the NE corner of the peak. From here, the summit is reached by climbing a chute of moderately-difficult rock and then slabs. Time: 6 hours from Royal Basin.

ROUTE 2. II, 4. Follow Route 1 until reaching the S side of the peak. From here, climb steep chimneys in the S face. Time: 6 hours from Royal Lake.

ROUTE 3. II, 4. First ascent 1961 by J. Munson and J. Parolini.

The route starts in Belvedere Basin immediately E of Mt. Clark (see Sundial, Route 2, for approach to the basin). From the basin, gain the lowest notch in the Clark-Adelaide ridge. Bear left and climb exposed slab for 400 ft., keeping to the N edge until the ridge is regained. Ascend SE to the summit. Time: 6 hours from Royal Lake.

ADELAIDE PEAK   ca. 7300

Located ⅓ mile north of Mt. Clark at the head of Belvedere Basin.

First ascent 1944 by A. Degenhardt and W. Degenhardt.

ROUTE. I, 3. From the S end of Belvedere Basin (see Sundial, Route 2, for approach), proceed to the N end of the basin and Adelaide Peak. Ascent is via the S side of the E ridge over slab and easy rock. Time: 4 hours from Royal Lake.

MT. WALKINSHAW (THE CITADEL)   7378

The northernmost summit in The Needles, this peak was recently renamed in honor of Robert B. Walkinshaw, prominent conservationist.

First ascent 1961 by J. Munson and J. Parolini.

ROUTE. I, 3. Leave the Royal Basin trail ca. 4½ miles from the Dungeness River trail (ca. 1½ miles below Royal Lake) near

Mt. Clark in The Needles (George W. Martin)

the point where the trail breaks out into open and relatively level meadows. Climb W ½ mile through small timber and brush. Continue climbing on easy scree slopes to the saddle between Walkinshaw and the Gray Wolf Ridge. Follow the ridge S and then ascend chimneys and slabs on the N side to the summit. Time: 4 hours from trail.

PETUNIA PEAK   ca. 6900
Located ca. ½ mile east of Royal Lake. This peak and its slopes are a fine vantage point for The Needles.

ROUTE. I, 2. Climb E from Royal Lake over talus and easy rock. Bear slightly N as elevation is gained to avoid rock outcroppings. The final few feet involve rock scrambling. Time: 3 hours from Royal Lake.

THE ROYAL SHAFT   ca. 6000
A prominent spire located ca. ½ mile southeast of Royal Lake on the shoulder of Petunia Peak.
First ascent 1962 by K. Hilton, J. Merkel, J. Munson, and J. Parolini.

ROUTE. I, 5.3, A1. Ascend SE directly from the lake to a platform on the E side of the spire. The 120-ft. climb to the top includes one aid pitch. Time: 3 hours from Royal Lake.

GRAY WOLF RIDGE   7218
A high barren ridge located between the Gray Wolf River and Royal Creek.

ROUTE. I, 2. The highest point is reached by climbing the SE slope after leaving the Royal Basin trail at the 3500-ft. level (ca. 2 miles up trail from Dungeness River). The Gray Wolf Ridge can also be reached by traversing S from Baldy.

BALDY   6797
Located between the Gray Wolf Ridge and Tyler Peak.

ROUTE. I, 1. Leave Forest Service road #295 (see Dungeness River approach) ca. ½ mile from its end (ca. 1½ miles past

Mueller Creek crossing). A cat trail can then be followed to meadows below the summit. Time: 3 hours from road.

TYLER PEAK   6364

Located on the Dungeness-Gray Wolf River divide 3 miles northeast of Gray Wolf Ridge.

First ascent by topographical survey party.

ROUTE. 1, 2. Leave the Dungeness River road (#295) at ca. 2950 ft. where it crosses Tyler Creek (ca. 6.7 miles above the first Dungeness River crossing). Climb W keeping to the N and above the creek bed to avoid heavy undergrowth. At about 3400 ft. contour into and across the creek. Ascend the left bank a short distance until a minor watercourse is reached. Angle left up this watercourse, which drains the E side of the ridge running SE from the summit. Climb to the obvious notch in this SE ridge. Cross through the notch and ascend NW over scree and heather to the easy summit. Time: 5 hours from road.

McCARTNEY PEAK   6728

Located at the head of the Lillian River.

ROUTE 1. 1, 2. Leave the Moose Lake-Grand Pass trail ca. 1 mile SW of Moose Lake (5 miles from Obstruction Point) and climb WSW to the 6000-ft. pass immediately S of Point 6753. An alternate approach to this pass is to leave the trail at Point 6536 (1.5 miles from Obstruction Point) and follow the open ridge S. Cross the pass into the Lillian River drainage and contour S ca. 2 miles on the W slope to the Lillian Glacier. Ascend the glacier to its head, then climb easy rock on the S side of the peak to the top. Time: 6 hours from Moose Lake.

ROUTE 2. 1, 2. From Dose Meadows (12.8 miles up the Dosewallips River trail) follow the Lost Pass-Cameron Pass trail to a point 200 yards S of Cameron Pass (2.8 miles from Dose Meadows). Leave the trail and follow the remains of an old trail NW along the ridge for ca. 2.5 miles to a small basin on the S side of McCartney Peak. From here, climb to the ridge and follow it NW to the easy summit. Time: 3 hours from Cameron Pass.

MT. ANGELES   6454

This peak, lying only 8 miles from tidewater, is located 2½ miles northeast of the Hurricane Ridge Visitor Center. It has several summits; the westernmost summit is the highest. This is a good practice climb because of accessibility and the availability of numerous routes in addition to those described here. Mt. Angeles is also a good winter climb.

ROUTE 1. I, 2. Leave the Hurricane Ridge road ca. 10.1 miles above the National Park boundary (ca. 2.9 miles below the Visitor Center) where the road crosses a major couloir descending from the S side of the peak. Follow the switchback trail up the right side of the creek to its junction with the 3-mile Mt. Angeles-Hurricane Ridge trail. Turn left, following the trail to Mt. Angeles saddle (¼ mile) and then ascend northerly keeping on the W side of the peak until just below the summit. Climb gully systems and rock to the top. Time: 3 hours from road.

ROUTE 2. I, 3. The route starts at the junction of the couloir trail (see Route 1) with the Mt. Angeles-Hurricane Ridge trail. Follow the Angeles-Hurricane Ridge trail a short distance westerly until it crosses the main couloir. Climb the couloir until it branches. Proceed up the right branch, which leads to the E side of the summit block. Time: 3 hours from road.

ROUTE 3. I, 2. From the junction of the couloir trail with the Mt. Angeles-Hurricane Ridge trail, turn right and follow the trail eastward and upward to the col immediately E of Mt. Angeles (Klahhane Saddle). From the col, climb NW, keeping to the S side of the ridge crest, to a point near the summit of the middle peak. From the middle peak, follow the ridge crest W to the main summit. Time: 3 hours from road.

ROUTE 4. I, 4. From the junction of the couloir trail with the Mt. Angeles-Hurricane Ridge trail, turn right and follow the trail eastward and upward to the col immediately E of Mt. Angeles (Klahhane Saddle). Cross the col and make a slightly descending traverse N (trail in summer) for ca. 20 minutes until a series of gully-chimneys is reached. Any of these may be ascended westerly to the ridge. The one farthest to the right is the most difficult. Once on the ridge, follow it S to the middle summit. From the middle summit, follow the ridge crest W to the main summit, which is climbed from the NE side. Time: 4 hours from car.

STEEPLE ROCK   5567

Located ca. 2 miles southwest of the Hurricane Ridge Visitor Center just above the Obstruction Point road. This accessible rock practice area offers a number of routes of varying difficulty.

Mt. Olympus-Bailey Range Group

Without question the king of the Olympics, the triple-crowned and glacier-clad 7965-ft. Mt. Olympus thrusts its crest far above the green rain forests on the Pacific slope of the Olympic Peninsula. Included in this group, in addition to Mt. Olympus and environs are the peaks of the Bailey Range, the isolated peaks surrounding the headwaters of the Soleduck River, and those near Olympic Hot Springs. The heavy glaciation of Mt. Olympus results from ocean-born southwesterly winds suddenly striking the Olympics, rising, and losing their moisture. Mt. Olympus has eight named glaciers of the valley type; the longest is some 3.8 miles in length. A number of small glaciers are located on the satellite peaks of Mt. Olympus and in the Bailey Range. This group offers the best snow and ice climbing found in the range. Small ridge and plateau lakes are plentiful in the upper Soleduck area.

Approaches

1. Elwha River-Olympic Hot Springs: This approach provides access to the Boulder Peak-Mt. Appleton area; to the north, central, and south end of the Bailey Range; and to the southeast side of the Olympus Massif.

The Elwha River-Olympic Hot Springs road leaves U.S. 101 9 miles SW of Port Angeles and climbs to the 2061-ft. Hot Springs in 11.8 miles. The Appleton Pass trail continues to 5000-ft. Appleton Pass (5 miles) and then drops to the Soleduck River trail (7.8 miles). A spur road leaves the Olympic Hot Springs road just beyond the Elwha Ranger Station (4.1 miles from U.S. 101) and continues up river 5 miles to Whiskey Bend and the Elwha River trail (see Southwestern Group, page 148, for details).

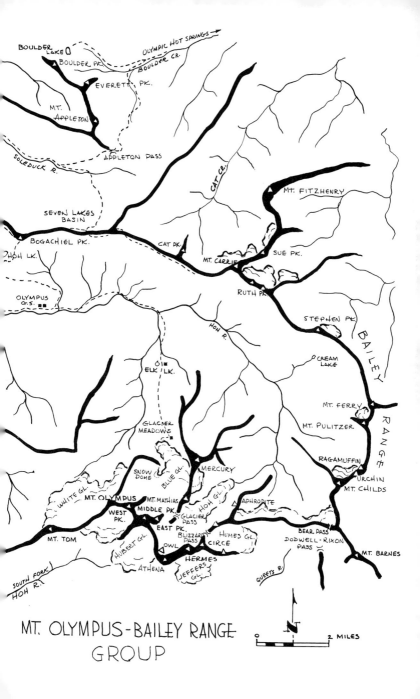

MT. OLYMPUS - BAILEY RANGE
GROUP

0   1   2 MILES

2. Soleduck River: This is the main approach to the High Divide and the north end of the Bailey Range.

The Soleduck River road leaves U.S. 101 30 miles W of Port Angeles just W of Lake Crescent and continues 14.2 miles to the Soleduck River trail (1.7 miles past Sol Duc Hot Springs). Shelters on the trail are located at Soleduck Falls (0.9 miles, 1900 ft.), Upper Soleduck (5.4 miles, 3200 ft.), and Soleduck Park (7.7 miles, 4500 ft.).

The Deer Lake-Bogachiel Peak trail branches from the Soleduck River trail at Soleduck Falls shelter. Shelters are also located at Deer Lake (3.9 miles from road end, 3500 ft.) and at Round and Lunch Lakes in Seven Lakes Basin (8.2 miles from road on 0.8 mile trail spur, 4300 ft.). The Deer Lake-Bogachiel Peak trail connects with the High Divide trail and the Hoh Lake trail (8.3 miles from road, 5200 ft.) near Bogachiel Peak. The High Divide trail meets the Soleduck River trail in 2.1 miles near Heart Lake, and then continues 3 additional miles to the S side of Cat Peak, providing the best northern access to the Bailey Range. The Hoh Lake trail (with a shelter at Hoh Lake, 4600 ft.) provides a 6.5-mile connection between the High Divide trail and the Hoh River trail.

3. Hoh River: This is the primary access to Mt. Olympus and environs.

The Hoh River road leaves U.S. 101 12.5 miles S of Forks and extends 19 miles to the Hoh River trail. The 16.6-mile Hoh River trail has shelters at Happy Four (5.3 miles, 820 ft.), Olympus (8.6 miles, 950 ft.), Elk Lake (14.0 miles, 2558 ft.), and Glacier Meadows (16.6 miles, 4200 ft.). The Tom Creek trail branches from the Hoh River trail at 2.7 miles, fords the river, and extends 1.2 miles to a shelter (700 ft.).

4. South Fork Hoh River: This approach can be used for a difficult access to Mt. Tom, Hoh Peak, and other seldom-visited peaks west of Mt. Olympus.

The South Fork Hoh River is reached via the Hoh-Clearwater Mainline Road which leaves U.S. 101 14.6 miles S of Forks at the Allen Logging Co. Follow the Hoh-Clearwater Mainline Road to a junction (stay left) 7.1 miles from U.S. 101. Stay left

Mt. Olympus—The Monarch of The Olympics (Dave Sicks)

again at a second junction (7.3 miles). From a third junction at Owl Creek (9.8 miles), stay left and continue to a fourth junction (turn left) at 14.8 miles; cross the South Fork Hoh River and follow a logging spur to its end at 17.8 miles. The South Fork Hoh River trail extends ca. 1.0 mile to Big Flat Shelter (732 ft.) and is maintained for another 2 miles.

5. Queets River: This approach is of limited value to climbers, but it does provide access to an interesting trail hike.

The Queets River road leaves U.S. 101 7 miles S of the town of Queets and extends 14 miles up river. The Queets River must be forded at road end to continue on the 15.5-mile Queets River trail. Shelters are located at Spruce Bottom (5 miles, 426 ft.), Bob Creek (11.1 miles, 580 ft.), and Pelton Creek (15.5 miles, 800 ft.).

Ranger Stations: Elwha (Elwha River road at 4.1 miles); Soleduck (Soleduck River road at 12.3 miles); Forks (U.S. 101); Queets (Queets River road at 12.5 miles); and Hoh (Hoh River road at 19 miles).

Campgrounds: U.S. 101: Fairholm, el. 550 ft. (W end of Lake Crescent); Kalaloch, el. 100 ft. (5 miles N of Queets on the ocean); Klahowya, el. 800 ft. (spur road 8 miles E of Sappho); Bogachiel State Park, el. 203 ft. (5 miles S of Forks on U.S. 101).

Elwha River-Olympic Hot Springs Road: Elwha, el. 300 ft. (3.0 miles from U.S. 101); Altaire, el. 400 ft. (4 miles); Olympic Hot Springs, el. 2060 ft. (11.8 miles).

Soleduck River Road: Soleduck, el. 1700 ft. (13 miles S of U.S. 101).

Hoh River Road: Hoh, el. 575 ft. (19 miles E of U.S. 101).

Queets River Road: Queets, el. 300 ft. (13.5 miles E of U.S. 101).

Vantage Points: Hurricane Ridge can be reached by road. Bogachiel Peak, Kloochman Rock, Dodger Point, Kimta Peak, and Mt. Storm King (overlooking Lake Crescent) can be reached by trail.

Maps: Olympic National Forest; USGS 30-minute Olympic National Park and Vicinity; *The Olympics in Relief*, published by Richard A. Pargeter and George W. Martin; the following 15-minute USGS quadrangles: Mt. Tom and Mt. Olympus; the following 7½-minute USGS quadrangles: Bogachiel Peak and Mt. Carrie.

References to two major passes, Blizzard Pass and Glacier Pass, are frequent in the route descriptions that follow. The most commonly used map of this area is the 15-minute USGS Mt. Olympus quadrangle, which shows the major pass between the Blue and Hoh Glaciers as Blizzard Pass. Glacier Pass is not represented on this map.

During the first annual Summer Outing of The Mountaineers in 1907, a group of climbers were caught in a blizzard while traversing the pass between the Humes and Hoh Glaciers. They bestowed the name of Blizzard on this pass, so in accordance with this footnote of history, and for the purpose of this guidebook, Blizzard Pass will be considered to be the major pass between the Humes and Hoh Glaciers. The major pass between the Blue and Hoh Glaciers will be referred to as Glacier Pass.

MT. OLYMPUS 7965

The monarch of the Olympics is located between the Hoh and Queets Rivers. It was named by John Meares in 1788 for the home of the Greek gods.

The West Peak is the highest, with the 7930-ft. Middle Peak closely rivaling it. The East Peak is slightly lower.

WEST PEAK 7965

First recognized ascent 1907 by L. A. Nelson and 10 members of The Mountaineers. There is serious doubt of the first-ascent claims of Col. B. F. Shaw and H. D. Clock (1854), Col. M. Simmons (1854), and B. J. Bretherton (1890).

Route 1. II, 3. A 16.6-mile trail climbs 3600 ft. to Glacier Meadows from the Hoh River Ranger Station. Another trail over the High Divide (5500 ft.) from the Soleduck River road (1900 ft.) joins the Hoh River trail (950 ft.) ½ mile E of Olympus Shelter, providing a variation in approach.

Mount Olympus

Blizzard Pass | Hermes | Mathias | Athena | East | Middle | West | Mt. Tom

Aries | | | Glacier Pass

Snow Dome

White Glacier

Blue Glacier

Mt. Carrie

Glacier Creek — Hoh Valley

Ruth Pk.

Sue Pk.

Hoh Valley

Hoh Valley

Hoh

Mount Olympus and
Bailey Range

From the end of the trail at Glacier Meadows (4200 ft.), follow way trail ca. ¼ mile to the Blue Glacier. Ascend the glacier, crossing to the W side. At about the 5500-ft. level, turn right and climb a snow slope to the crest of the Snow Dome (6600 ft.) keeping left of the rock buttress. As an alternate route, the rock can be climbed directly to the Snow Dome. About 3 hours are required to reach the Snow Dome from Glacier Meadows. From the Snow Dome, proceed through a 7200-ft. snow pass S 20° E. Turn right and climb WSW to the top of the false summit. Drop to the saddle between the false summit and the West Peak and climb steep snow to the NE side of the rock summit; from here, the top is reached after a short steep rock climb. Time: 7 hours from Glacier Meadows.

ROUTE 2. II, 3. From Elwha Basin, climb the Elwha Snow-finger to 4850-ft. Dodwell-Rixon Pass (see Southwestern Group, page 148). Descend into Queets Basin where camp may be made at the W edge of the basin next to the Humes Glacier (4500 ft.). Ascend easy rock on the S edge of the glacier, bypassing the ice-fall, and continue up the glacier to Blizzard Pass (6100 ft.).

Mount Olympus-West Peak
from Snow Dome

Drop 650 ft. to the Hoh Glacier on a left-angling descent. Climb W on the Hoh Glacier to 6800 ft. and then NW, climbing over the Middle Peak and traversing to the false summit described in Route 1. Time: 8 hours from campsite in Queets Basin.

ROUTE 3 (WEST RIDGE). II, 5.3. First ascent 1964 by G. Maykut, L. Miller, and J. Witte.
From the Snow Dome (see Route 1), proceed to the N side of the W ridge at its lowest point. Climb the ridge crest to a large vertical step separating two shallow gullies. Traverse right and climb a 100-ft. Class 5.3 pitch. Continue just below the ridge crest on easy rock to a notch 400 ft. higher. Bypass gendarmes on a ledge on the N side of the ridge to snow at the base of the summit pyramid and continue to the top. Time: 6 hours from Glacier Meadows.

MIDDLE PEAK   7930
First ascent 1907 by B. H. Browne, W. G. Clarke, G. W. Humes, and H. C. Parker.
ROUTE 1. II, 3. Go through a 7200-ft. snow pass S 20° E from the top of the Snow Dome (see Route 1, West Peak) to the Middle Peak over an easy glacier slope. Climb the W side via 100 ft. of rock. Time: 7 hours from Glacier Meadows.

ROUTE 2. II, 3. Follow Route 2, East Peak, but stay S of East Peak, continuing W to Middle Peak.

EAST PEAK   7780
First ascent 1899 by J. McGlone, a member of the Dodwell-Rixon survey party.
ROUTE 1. II, 3. From Route 1, Middle Peak, go over the top of the Middle Peak and ascend the SW side of the East Peak.

ROUTE 2. II, 3. Climb from Glacier Pass (6200 ft.) by swinging southwesterly around rock buttresses, beneath hanging ice which presents possible avalanche danger, and then up the SE side.

OLYMPUS TRAVERSE
A traverse of the three main peaks of Olympus may be done by climbing West Peak first, then proceeding to Middle Peak, and

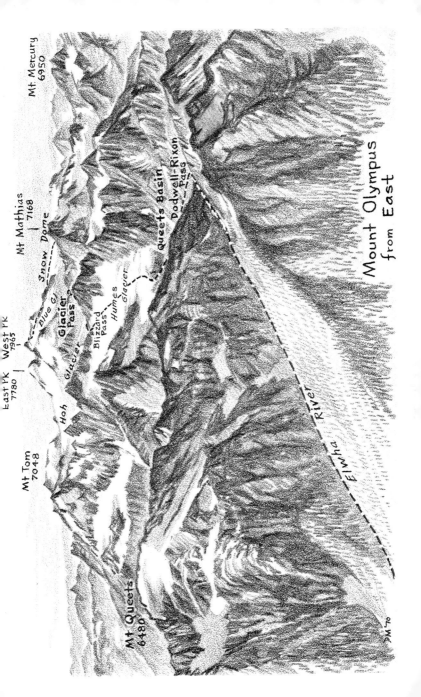

Mt Queets 6480

Mt Tom 7048

East Pk 7780 | West Pk 7965

Mt Mathias 7168

Mt Mercury 6950

Hoh Glacier

Glacier Pass

Blue G.

Snow Dome

Blizzard Pass

Humes Glacier

Queets Basin

Dodwell-Rixon Pass

Elwha River

Mount Olympus from East

DM '70

thence to East Peak, returning to Glacier Meadows through Glacier Pass.

MT. TOM   7048

Located 2 miles west of the summit of Mt. Olympus at the west end of the upper White Glacier.

First ascent 1914 by E. Meany and a group of Boy Scouts including T. Martin, for whom the peak was named.

ROUTE 1. II, 3. From the Snow Dome of Mt. Olympus (see Route 1, Mt. Olympus), bear SW keeping close to the West Peak of Mt. Olympus. Cross the crest of a rock ridge running W from the Mt. Olympus summit, just before it drops sharply to the valley. Proceed SW on the crest of the adjoining right-angle ridge for several hundred yards. Turn right into a shallow gully just before this latter ridge breaks sharply, and descend the gully down a steep rock face. Descend the steep snow slope at the bottom of the gully to reach the White Glacier. Traverse the glacier westerly to the summit of Mt. Tom, or bear left to gain the rock ridge leading up to the summit. The highest point is the lefthand peak as seen from the White Glacier. Time: 9 hours from Glacier Meadows.

ROUTE 2. II, 3. From the end of the Tom Creek trail (900 ft.), proceed up the creek through brush to the headwall (ca. 6 miles). Bear left and climb steep, timbered slopes to timberline, where an excellent campsite exists at lakes on a large bench (5100 ft.). From this bench, the W side of the White Glacier can be easily reached, and the glacier ascended to the summit.

The South Fork Hoh River trail offers a third possibility for an approach to the Mt. Tom area; however, this route is long and difficult.

MT. MATHIAS (APOLLO)   7168

Located between the Blue and Hoh Glaciers northeast of Glacier Pass. Originally named Apollo, this peak was officially renamed in honor of F. W. Mathias, a prominent Grays Harbor area mountaineer and conservationist, as a result of efforts by the Grays Harbor Olympians of Aberdeen, Washington.

First ascent 1957 by Y. Eriksson and J. Hawkins.

ROUTE 1. II, 4. Ascend a steep glacier finger leading from the Blue Glacier to a high col between Mathias and a sharp pinnacle just NE of Glacier Pass. Passage of this finger may be difficult late in the season due to bergschrunds. Attack the steep ridge to Mathias directly, working onto ledges on the W face as steep pitches near the summit are reached. Eventually gain the opposite ridge just below the summit. The climb is on exposed rotten rock. Time: 6 hours from Glacier Meadows.

ROUTE 2. II, 4. Ascend shallow gullies from the Blue Glacier to the Mercury-Mathias col. Descend the E side of the ridge 200 ft. to a snowfield. Climb S, swinging around a prominent buttress, then regain the ridge crest and proceed to the summit. Time: 8 hours from Glacier Meadows.

MERCURY   6950

A triangular peak located 1 mile north of Mt. Mathias.
First ascent 1955 by R. Hubley.

ROUTE 1. I, 3. Proceed to Mathias-Mercury col (Mathias, Route 2) and climb N directly up the ridge to the Mercury summit. Time: 5 hours from Glacier Meadows.

A fine climber's high camp, sometimes called Camp Pan, is located ca. 300 ft. above the Hoh Glacier on a rocky promontory at the north edge of the slope which leads from the Hoh Glacier to Blizzard Pass (Hoh-Humes Pass). This camp may be reached in ca. 4 hours from Glacier Meadows and is a good central location from which the remaining Mt. Olympus area climbs may be made.

ATHENA (SOUTH PEAK, OLYMPUS)   ca. 7350

This is the highest point at the south edge of the head of the Hoh Glacier.
First ascent 1940 by E. Johnson and G. Martin.

ROUTE. II, 3. From Camp Pan, descend to the Hoh Glacier and then climb to its head. Bear SSE along a large snow crest, passing W of Athena's Owl, and continue along the crest to the base of Athena. Circle to the right, and ascend easy rock slightly exposed in places. Reach the summit by turning the N arête on the left just below the summit. This peak can also be reached from the Snow Dome and from Queets Basin, as described in the routes on Mt. Olympus. Time: 5 hours from Camp Pan.

ATHENA'S OWL   ca. 7000

A sharp, double-pronged nunatak located in the Hoh Glacier north of Athena.

First ascent 1963 by W. Leggett and G. Maykut.

ROUTE. II, 3. Proceed as for Athena, but leave the snow crest when the W side of the Owl is reached. This short climb is made from the W side after descending a wind-carved moat which describes an arc around the N, W, and S sides of the Owl. Ascend rock to just below the N "ear," where a horizontal traverse leads to the notch between the N and S "ears." The knife-edged summit of the higher S "ear" is reached in one rope lead from the notch by following the E side of the ridge just below the crest. This climb is not difficult, but it is exposed. Time: 5 hours from Camp Pan.

HERMES   ca. 6860

This sharp rock peak is on the south margin of the Hoh Glacier, approximately ½ mile west of Circe.

First ascent 1955 by R. Hubley and E. LaChapelle.

ROUTE. II, 3. From Camp Pan, follow the E edge of the Hoh Glacier S to the base of Hermes. Ascend steep, broken ice to the col NE of the Hermes summit. Crossing the schrund may be very difficult late in the season. Ascend a sharp ridge on easy rotten rock W to the summit. Time: 4 hours from Camp Pan.

CIRCE   6874

Located at the junction of three rock ridges which separate the Hoh, Humes, and Jeffers Glaciers.

ROUTE. II, 2. From Camp Pan, climb to Blizzard Pass and follow a gentle ridge S to the summit. Time: 2 hours from Camp Pan.

ARIES   ca. 6800

Located ca. ½ mile northeast of Circe.

    ROUTE. II, 3. From Camp Pan, proceed NE to the NW side of Aries; climb to summit via mixed snow and rock. Difficulty with a bergschrund may be encountered. Time: 3 hours from Camp Pan.

APHRODITE   6254

Located ca. 1½ miles northeast of Circe.

    ROUTE. II, 3. From Camp Pan, contour NE ca. 1 mile, keeping above the Hoh Glacier to the W side of Aphrodite where the summit may be gained by easy snow and a rock scramble. A bergschrund may exist late in the season. Time: 4 hours from Camp Pan.

ICARUS   ca. 6200

A double-spired peak located ca. ¾ mile east of Circe on the south edge of the Humes Glacier. Both spires appear to be of equal elevation.

First ascent 1966 by B. West and M. West.

    ROUTE. II, 3. From Camp Pan, climb ca. 500 ft. through Blizzard Pass and contour S and E around the Humes Glacier (ca. 1 mile). Circle around the N side of Icarus to the E face of the E spire. Climb gully and chimney systems to the summit on loose rock. Time: 3 hours from Camp Pan.

THE VALHALLAS   6038

This interesting but little known group of peaks is centered 3½ miles southwest of Mt. Olympus, between the Queets River and the South Fork Hoh River. Resembling a miniature Bugaboos, these peaks are an extension of Mt. Olympus' southwest ridge. The central and highest peaks lie in a horseshoe around the Geri-Freki Glacier, whose melt waters provide one of the main sources of the South Fork Hoh River. Only the central peaks are described in the following paragraphs. They are listed in order clockwise around the Geri-Freki Glacier starting with Thor in the northeast. The ridge system continues southwest past Woden, the highest summit, to *Pelton Peak*, with several unnamed peaks lying beween. The peaks of The Valhallas are named after the gods of Norse Mythology.

The area can be approached from the South Fork Hoh River, from the Queets River, or from Mt. Olympus. The South Fork Hoh River approach is the easiest for the central peaks and is described in detail.

For road access details see the South Fork Hoh River approach. From the road end, follow a maintained trail for 3½ miles, passing Big Flat Shelter inside the Park boundary. From the end of the trail, continue up the north side of the river for another 9 miles to a large boulder field. The main peaks of The Valhallas are approximately one mile southeast of this point. Continue up river over the moss covered boulders. Immediately past the boulder field, cross the river and climb the steep wooded slopes on the left side of Valkyrie Creek. Keeping well left of the creek, attain the ridge and then climb it to alpine meadows at 4400 feet where camp can be made on the crest. From camp, contour into the Valkyrie Creek basin and then climb up a steep couloir to the col between Frigga on the left and Baldur on the right. The following route descriptions start at this col, which is approximately 45 minutes from camp.

THOR   ca. 5950

Located above the lower southeast side of the Geri-Freki Glacier approximately ⅔ mile from the Baldur-Frigga col.

First ascent 1971 by R. Beckett, D. Haley, G. Kelsey, M. Lennox, D. Michael, D. Stevens, and R. Yekel.

ROUTE. II, 3. From the Baldur-Frigga col, contour to the glacier, cross it to the SE and climb to the Thor-Loki Spire notch. Climb a rotten rock couloir to the summit. Time: 1½ hours from the Baldur-Frigga col.

LOKI SPIRE   ca. 5700

A 300-foot pinnacle located immediately southwest of Thor.

First ascent 1971 by R. Beckett, D. Haley, G. Kelsey, M. Lennox, D. Michael, D. Stevens, and R. Yekel.

ROUTE. II, 3. Climb rotten rock from the Hugin-Loki col after an approach for Thor. The last 10 ft. are climbed flagpole fashion. Time: ½ hour from the Hugin-Loki col.

HUGIN   ca. 5990

Located above the southeast side of the Geri-Freki Glacier approximately ⅔ mile from the Baldur-Frigga col. It is the peak immediately east of peak 6038 (Woden) on the 1956 Mt. Olympus quadrangle.

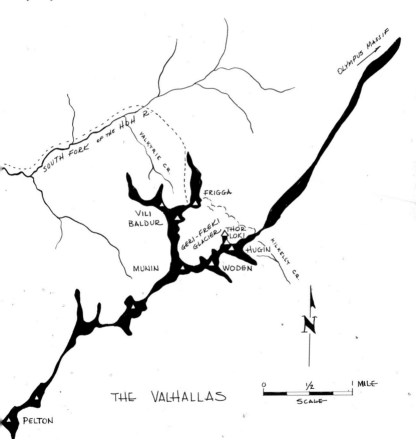

THE VALHALLAS

First ascent 1966 by W. Howarth, E. Labistida, I. Lindgren and J. Wall.

ROUTE. II, 2. From the Baldur-Frigga col, cross the glacier to the SE keeping to the left of Woden. Scramble up rotten rock on the NW side to the summit. Time: 1 hour from the Baldur-Frigga col.

WODEN   6038

This peak, the highest in The Valhallas, is located above the upper southeast side of the Geri-Freki Glacier slightly over ½ mile from the Baldur-Frigga col.

First ascent 1966 by E. Labistida and I. Lindgren.

ROUTE. II, 4. From the Baldur-Frigga col, cross the glacier to the SE and then ascend a snowfield to the NE corner of the peak. Climb a jam crack and then traverse to the left under an overhang. Next, ascend a short chimney to the summit ridge. Either climb the ridge to the summit or traverse around to the S face and climb one Class 4 pitch. Time: 1½ hours from the Baldur-Frigga col.

MUNIN   ca. 6000

Located near the head of the Geri-Freki Glacier immediately west of Woden. It is approximately ⅔ mile from the Baldur-Frigga col.

First ascent 1966 by E. Labistida and I. Lindgren.

ROUTE. II, 4. From the Baldur-Frigga col, ascend the glacier southerly to the Munin-Woden saddle. An interesting rock scramble along the ridge leads to the summit. Time: 1½ hours from the Baldur-Frigga col.

BALDUR   ca. 5750

Located above the upper northwest side of the Geri-Freki Glacier immediately southwest of the Baldur-Frigga col.

First ascent 1971 by R. Beckett, D. Haley, G. Kelsey, M. Lennox, D. Michael, H. Pinsch, D. Stevens and R. Yekel.

ROUTE. II, 2. From the Baldur-Frigga col, ascend the NW side of the glacier around the base of Baldur and then climb to the Munin-Baldur saddle. Traverse the easy ridge to the summit. Time: 1 hour from the Baldur-Frigga col.

FRIGGA   ca. 5300

Located immediately northeast of the Baldur-Frigga col.

First ascent 1971 by R. Beckett, D. Haley, G. Kelsey, M. Lennox, D. Michael, H. Pinsch, D. Stevens and R. Yekel.

ROUTE. II, 2. Climb from the Baldur-Frigga col via a short but exposed scramble on rotten rock. In late summer the start onto the rock may be difficult. Time: ½ hour from the Baldur-Frigga col.

BAILEY RANGE

This long curving chain of peaks, paralleling the upper Hoh River canyon, contains summits averaging 6500 ft. elevation. Mt. Carrie, at 6995 ft., is the highest. This isolated range will be presented from north to south through and including Mt. Childs. The southwest slope of the range, bordering the Hoh, presents generally smooth sides, but on the northeast the range is roughly indented and has numerous small glaciers. Named by the Press Party for William E. Bailey, proprietor of *The Seattle Press.*

MT. FITZHENRY   ca. 6050

Located between Cat Creek and Long Creek at the north end of the Bailey Range.

ROUTE. II, 2. From the dam at the N end of Lake Mills, take the 2-mile trail which ends at Boulder Creek. From here, follow the lake shore, keeping high to avoid cliffs. Cross Cat Creek and ascend the dry wooded ridge separating Cat Creek from Fitzhenry Creek, to the 5948-ft. false summit. Drop slightly and continue on to the true summit ½ mile distant. Time: 8 hours up, 6 hours down.

This route may be shortened somewhat by making the approach to Cat Creek via boat on Lake Mills. Fitzhenry has been climbed from Long Creek; however, no details are currently available.

SUE PEAK   ca. 6950

Located ¾ mile northeast of Mt. Carrie.

First ascent 1963 by D. Baker, J. Christiansen, R. Etten, and D. Pruitt.

Descending from the Mt. Olympus Summit to the Snow Dome
(George W. Martin)

ROUTE. II, 3. From the summit of Mt. Fitzhenry, descend the ridge SW to a saddle, and drop several hundred feet on the W side of the saddle. Proceed SE to the glacier on the N side of Sue Peak. Ascend the glacier ca. 1500 ft. to the highest of several rocky summits and scramble to the top. Time: 3 full days for the round-trip from Lake Mills. See Fitzhenry approach.

CAT PEAK   ca. 5940

A double-summited peak located on the Hoh River-Cat Creek divide.

ROUTE. I, 1. From ca. ½ mile before the end of the trail (see Mt. Carrie), climb N past the 5600-ft. false summit to the top. Time: 2 hours from the trail.

MT. CARRIE   6995

The central and highest peak in the Bailey Range, located on the Long Creek-Hoh River divide. Named by T. Rixon during the first USGS survey of forest resources, 1898–1900, for Carrie Jones, his wife-to-be.

ROUTE. I, 2. The best approach is from the end of the Soleduck River road, taking the trail through Soleduck Park to the High Divide. Here a branch trail contours E above the Hoh River valley ca. 3 miles to its end at 5100 ft. between Cat Peak and Mt. Carrie. From the end of this trail, climb to the ridge top (elevation gain ca. 200 ft.) and proceed E along the narrow ridge crest called the "Catwalk." Continue NE along the summit ridge, keeping to the right side on easy shale and heather to the false summit. The main summit is farther E. Time: 5 hours from camp at Heart Lake. (A fine campsite exists ca. ½ mile before the end of the trail; however, water must be obtained from a spring at the end of the trail.)

RUTH PEAK   ca. 6850

A twin-spired peak located 1 mile east-southeast of Mt. Carrie. First ascent 1961 by B. Brown, R. Etten, and V. Nelson.

ROUTE. II, 3. From the summit of Mt. Carrie traverse E down Carrie Glacier for ¾ mile, then climb a steep glacial finger ca. 500 ft. to the ridge crest W of the summit. Follow ledge systems on the S side of the W spire to rotten gully systems leading to the summit. Time: 3 hours from the summit of Mt. Carrie.

STEPHEN PEAK   ca. 6430

Located on the Hoh River-Long Creek divide 2 miles southeast of Ruth Peak.

First recorded ascent 1961 by K. Heathershaw, D. Waali, and R. Wood.

ROUTE. II, 2. From upper Cream Lake Basin, ascend steep heather to the ridge crest at the SE end of the massif. Contour W on snowfields below the ragged crest, and climb a narrow ridge to the summit at the NE end of the peak. Time: 4 hours.

MT. FERRY   6157

Located 2 miles southeast of Cream Lake.

Named by the Press Party for Elisha P. Ferry, Washington State's first governor.

ROUTE. II, 2. The approach can be made from Ludden Peak, from Mt. Carrie, or from Bear Pass near Dodwell-Rixon Pass. The final ascent is easy from either the S or E side.

LUDDEN PEAK   5828

Located near the south end of the Long Creek-Elwha River divide.

ROUTE. I, 2. From 2 miles up the Elwha River trail, follow the Long Ridge trail to Dodger Point (13.3 miles from Whiskey Bend). Next, follow a way trail along the ridge SW, and climb to the summit. Time: 2 hours from Dodger Point.

MT. SCOTT   5913

Located 1 mile south of Ludden Peak.

ROUTE. I, 2. Follow the trail from Dodger Point ca. 2 miles to its end just E of Ludden Peak. Drop ca. 100 ft. to avoid the cliffs of Ludden's E face, and then climb on elk trails to the saddle between Ludden and Scott where a fine campsite exists. Final ascent is via the N ridge of Scott. Time: 5 hours from Dodger Point.

MT. PULITZER (SNAGTOOTH) 6283

Located ½ mile southwest of Mt. Ferry. Named by the Press Party for Joseph Pulitzer, publisher of the *New York World*.

ROUTE. II, 3. Ascend the exposed E ridge over extremely splintered rock. Time: 1 hour from Mt. Ferry.

THE RAGAMUFFIN AND THE URCHIN ca. 6000

These pinnacles are located ½ mile northeast of Mt. Childs.
First ascent 1961 by K. Heathershaw and D. Waali.

ROUTE. Both pinnacles can be climbed on their N ridges. Time for each: 3 hours from Bear Pass.

MT. CHILDS 6205

Located 1½ miles northeast of Bear Pass, at the extreme south end of the Bailey Range. Named by the Press Party for George Washington Childs, publisher of the *Philadelphia Ledger*.
First recorded ascent 1961 by K. Heathershaw, D. Waali, and R. Wood.

ROUTE. II, 2. Traverse to the E side of the peak from Bear Pass and ascend talus to the summit. Time: 2 hours from Bear Pass.

BOULDER PEAK ca. 5600

A pyramidal peak on the Boulder Creek-North Fork Soleduck River divide, 3 miles west of Olympic Hot Springs.

ROUTE. I, 1. Take the 3.4-mile trail from Olympic Hot Springs to Boulder Lake (4350 ft.) just NE of the peak. From the lake, ascend steep heather and easy rock slopes to the top. Time: 4 hours from Olympic Hot Springs.

MT. APPLETON ca. 6000

Located on the Boulder Creek-Soleduck River divide.

ROUTE. I, 1. Follow the Olympic Hot Springs-Appleton Pass trail ca. 4 miles to where it crosses the South Fork of Boulder Creek. Leave the trail and climb W to a 5800-ft. saddle between Mt. Appleton and a slightly higher but unnamed peak to the S. Continue N to the summit. Time: 5 hours from Olympic Hot Springs.

Southwestern Group

Around the headwaters of the Elwha River is a fine group of peaks averaging 6400 ft. in elevation. At the head of the Elwha River is the Elwha Snowfinger, which leads to Dodwell-Rixon Pass and the Queets Basin. This pass to the high country was used by the original survey party in 1888-1900. The lowest trans-Olympic pass, the 3602-ft. Low Divide between the Elwha and the North Fork Quinault drainages, was crossed by the Press Party Expedition in 1890. Mt. Meany (6695 ft.), named in honor of Edmond Meany, is the central peak. Dr. Meany was a long-time President of The Mountaineers in Seattle and a Professor of History at the University of Washington. Of this group, Mt. Christie, Mt. Seattle, and Mt. Queets support glaciers on their northern sides.

The peaks will be covered generally up the Elwha and down the Quinault. Side-trips will be covered from nearest campsites.

Approaches

1. North Fork Quinault River: This is the shortest approach for Mt. Christie and the Meany-Queets-Noyes Massif. It is also the primary approach for the peaks of Kimta, Lawson, and Zindorf.

The North Fork Quinault River road leaves U.S. 101 about 1 mile N of Amanda Park and extends 18.6 miles to the North Fork Quinault Ranger Station and Campground (500 ft.). The North Fork Quinault River trail continues to Low Divide and drops to join the Elwha River trail at Chicago Camp. There are shelters at Francis Creek (7.0 miles, 1000 ft.), Twelve Mile (12.3 miles, 2000 ft.), and at Low Divide (16.1 miles, 3600 ft.). The Three Lakes-Skyline trail leaves the North Fork Quinault

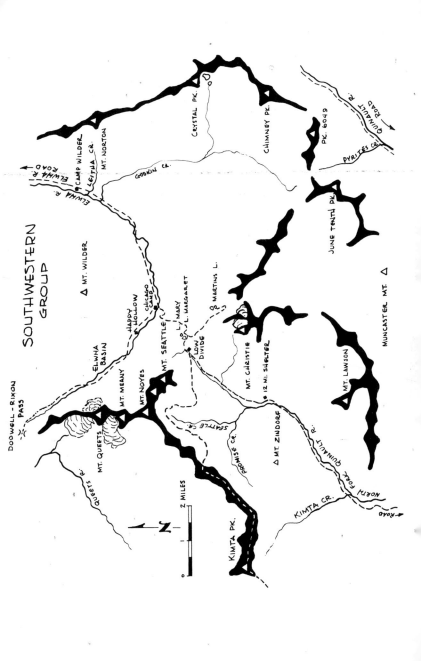

River road at North Fork Quinault Campground and eventually rejoins the North Fork Quinault River trail near Low Divide. Shelters are located at Three Lakes (6.6 miles, 3600 ft.) and Three Prune Creek (10.9 miles, 3600 ft.).

2. Quinault River: This approach is used mainly to reach the Enchanted Valley peaks including Crystal Peak, Chimney Peak, June 10th Peak, and Muncaster Mountain. Though long, it can also be used as a western approach for Mt. Anderson and environs (see Dosewallips Group, page 77).

The Quinault River road leaves U.S. 101 ½ mile SE of Amanda Park near Lake Quinault. It passes along the S side of the lake, follows the S side of the river, and ends 21.6 miles from U.S. 101 (3 miles upriver from the Graves Creek Ranger Station). The Quinault River trail continues 15.6 miles through the Enchanted Valley to join with the Dosewallips trail at Anderson Pass (see Dosewallips Group, page 72). There are shelters at O'Neil Creek (4.8 miles, 1179 ft.) and in the Enchanted Valley (Enchanted Valley Chalet: 10.8 miles, 1957 ft.). There is also a shelter a short distance E of Anderson Pass, affectionately known as "Siberia."

3. Elwha River: This approach is gentle and can be used to reach most of the peaks of this group. It is the most practical approach for Mt. Norton, Mt. Dana, Mt. Barnes, and Mt. Wilder. It is also the approach for the Bailey Range (see Mt. Olympus-Bailey Range Group, page 141).

The Elwha River road leaves U.S. 101 8 miles SW of Port Angeles and follows the E side of the river upstream for 9.1 miles to the end of a spur road at Whiskey Bend. The main road crosses the river just beyond the Elwha Ranger Station (4.1 miles) and continues to Olympic Hot Springs, an additional 8 miles. From Olympic Hot Springs, a trail leads 5 miles to join the Soleduck River trail via Appleton Pass (covered in Mt. Olympus-Bailey Range Group, page 124). The Elwha River trail, starting at Whiskey Bend, extends approximately 30 miles to Elwha Basin below Dodwell-Rixon Pass. This is the eastern approach to the Olympus Massif and the southern approach to the Bailey Range. Shelters are located at Michael's Ranch (2.3 miles, 1100 ft.), Lillian River (4.7 miles, 1300 ft.), Mary Falls (8.8

miles, 1200 ft.), Canyon Camp (10.5 miles, 1400 ft.), Elkhorn (11.5 miles, 1500 ft.), Stony Point (11.7 miles, 1500 ft.), Remann's (12.8 miles, 1500 ft.), Hayes River (16.8 miles, 1600 ft.), Wilder (20.9 miles, 1900 ft.), Chicago (25.8 miles, 2200 ft.), and Happy Hollow (26.8 miles, 2400 ft.). A trail leaving at Hayes River joins the Dosewallips River trail via Hayden Pass (see Dosewallips Group, page 72). The trail from Chicago Camp to Low Divide, joining the Elwha trail with the North Fork Quinault trail, is 2½ miles long and quite steep. There are additional fisherman campsites along the Elwha trail and frequent places to obtain good drinking water from springs and streams as well as the river.

Ranger Stations: Quinault (South Shore Lake Quinault-USFS), Graves Creek (Quinault River road-NPS), Quinault (North Fork Quinault River road-NPS), North Fork (North Fork Quinault River road-NPS), and Elwha (Elwha River road-NPS). Guard Stations: Elkhorn, Hayes River, and Low Divide.

Campgrounds: Quinault River Road: Olallie, el. 200 ft. (1 mile E of U.S. 101); Willaby, el. 200 ft. (2 miles); Falls Creek, el. 200 ft. (2½ miles); Graves Creek, el. 550 ft. (18.5 miles).
North Fork Road: July Creek, el. 200 ft. (3.5 miles E of U.S. 101); North Fork, el. 500 ft. (18.6 miles).
Elwha River Road: Elwha, el. 300 ft. (3.0 miles S of U.S. 101); Altaire, el. 500 ft. (4.1 miles).

Vantage Points: Kloochman Rock (Queets River) and Mt. Colonel Bob (E of Lake Quinault). Both can be reached by trail.

Maps: Olympic National Forest; USGS 30-minute Olympic National Park and Vicinity; *The Olympics in Relief*, published by Richard A. Pargeter and George W. Martin; the following 15-minute USGS quadrangles: Mt. Olympus, Mt. Angeles, Mt. Christie, and Mt. Steel.

MT. NORTON   6319
Located toward the north end of the ridge separating the Hayes River from the Elwha River, 2½ miles east of Camp Wilder.
First recorded ascent 1947 by P. Cummings.

ROUTE 1. I, 2. Leave the Elwha River trail ½ mile S of Camp Wilder after crossing Leitha Creek. Follow the ridge E about 2 miles to open meadows at ca. 5500 ft. Turn N to gain the ridge crest which leads to the summit. Time: 4 hours from Camp Wilder.

ROUTE 2. I, 2. Climb the wooded ridge paralleling the trail to Camp Wilder after leaving the trail at Hayes River Bridge and climbing Norton's N ridge to a basin where camp may be made. From here, climb the sharp ridge first on the E side, then cross to the W side past several pinnacles to the summit.

CRYSTAL PEAK   6896

Located on the Hayes River-Godkin Creek divide 2 miles west of West Peak (Anderson Massif).

ROUTE 1. II, 2. Leave the Elwha River trail ½ mile S of Camp Wilder on the ridge crest immediately after crossing Leitha Creek. Follow the ridge E about 2 miles to open meadows at ca. 5500 ft. Follow elk trails SE along a series of lakes and a bench system ca. 3½ miles to Lower Crystal Lake (5700 ft.) where good campsites and wood are available. Climb a talus slope NE to a saddle, bypassing a waterfall that spills from the upper lake, and traverse to the main ridge. The summit is reached by continuing N via the ridge or gully systems. Time: 3 hours from Lower Crystal Lake.

ROUTE 2. II, 3. From the saddle between Godkin Creek and the West Fork of Anderson Creek (see Route 2, Chimney Peak), the S ridge can be followed by contouring the first peak on the W side and the second peak on the E. Join Route 1 at Upper Crystal Lake. Time: 8 hours from Enchanted Valley Chalet.

CHIMNEY PEAK   6911

Located on the ridge between Godkin Creek and the Quinault River, 1½ miles north of Enchanted Valley Chalet.
First known ascent 1941 by T. Nelson of USGS.

ROUTE 1. II, 3. Locate the abandoned trail on the N edge of Pyrites Creek (7½ miles from road end on Quinault River trail). Follow the trail NW ca. 1½ miles until it peters out, and continue ascent toward head of valley. Camp can be made at timberline on the easternmost tributary of Pyrites Creek, 4 hours from Quinault River trail. Climb above timberline, contour the S side of Peak 6049, and cross through the 4800-ft. pass just E of Peak 6049. Drop ca. 1000 ft. to where an easy but long traverse can be made to the central snowfield of Chimney's SW face, staying below several rock ribs. Climb the 40° snowfield to gain the S ridge just below the summit, and continue to the top over ground covered with quartz crystals. Time: 5½ hours from camp.

ROUTE 2. II, 4. First known ascent 1962 by D. Pargeter and R. Pargeter.

From the Quinault River trail at the confluence of Anderson Creek and the Quinault River (13 miles from road end), cross the river and follow Anderson Creek 0.4 mile to where it branches. Continue up the left branch, gaining 3500 ft. in 1.7 miles to the ridge overlooking Godkin Creek. Proceed S 0.2 mile to a small summit at ca. 6300 ft. and continue S, contouring a steep exposed snow slope on the E side of the ridge, and rotten rock for another 0.2 mile. Rounding the S side of a rock shoulder, the terrain eases to gentle snow slopes. Contour these SW beneath a 6700-ft. peak for 0.7 mile, passing a small tarn with good water. Proceed SW to the summit, gaining 850 ft. via the snow of the N ridge. Time: 8 hours from Enchanted Valley Chalet.

PEAK 6049 6049
Located on the Godkin Creek-Quinault River divide, 1½ miles southwest of Chimney Peak.

ROUTE. I, 3. From camp (Route 1, Chimney Peak), scramble up the false summits of the W ridge through sharp upthrusting shale and contorted fir and cedar trees to the top. Time: 2 hours from camp.

JUNE 10TH PEAK 6019
Located ca. 1 mile southwest of the headwaters of Pyrites Creek, on the northwest side of the Enchanted Valley.

First ascent 1963 by J. Ansell, E. Fukushima, C. Howard, and R. McConnell.

ROUTE. I, 2. From camp (Route 1, Chimney Peak), traverse on elk trails to just below the 4850-ft. pass at the head of Pyrites Creek. Continue around the head of Pyrites Creek to a 5300-ft. col on the shoulder of the peak. Ascend the ridge to the summit. Time: 3 hours from camp.

MUNCASTER MOUNTAIN 5910

A massive mountain located 2½ miles northwest of O'Neil Creek Shelter, on the Quinault River-Rustler Creek divide.
First known ascent 1941 by T. Nelson of USGS.

ROUTE 1. II, 3. From 2 miles up the Quinault River trail (950 ft.), ascend the ridge on the E side of Fire Creek to timberline (4700 ft.). Go past a 5624-ft. summit on its W side to a 5150-ft. notch in the NW ridge. Drop a few hundred feet to the E side of an open basin and contour N by W to regain the ridge at a 5000-ft. saddle SE of Mt. Muncaster. Traverse right to the NE face, and ascend the snowfield to the summit.
A somewhat more difficult variation involves contouring up the SE ridge from the 5000-ft. notch over sharp, weak shale to a gully on the W side. Follow the gully to the summit plateau.

ROUTE 2. II, 3. From camp (Route 1, Chimney Peak) traverse past June 10th Peak on the Rustler Creek side of the ridge. Time: 10 hours.

MT. DANA 6209

Located on the Elwha-Goldie River divide.

ROUTE 1. I, 2. From Happy Hollow Shelter, 1 mile up the Elwha River from Chicago Camp, continue upriver on trail a few hundred yards to gain easier access to slopes leading N. Follow elk trails up a spur ridge 1 mile to the crest of the main ridge joining Mt. Barnes and Mt. Dana at a silver forest burn. The ridge loops around the headwaters of the Goldie River, with Mt. Wilder on a spur separating two forks. From this crest, follow the ridge NE via game trails past Mt. Wilder to the summit. Time: 5 hours from camp.

ROUTE 2. II, 2. First recorded ascent 1968 by R. Tabor, R. Yeates, and D. Yeates of USGS.

Ford the Elwha River near the first flat N of Hayes River Guard Station, ascending the NE ridge to about 4500 ft. Traverse the N face W, staying below cliffs to a campsite in a meadow at ca. 4700 ft. Ascend a snowfield and chute to a second basin. Climb W to the N ridge and follow it to the summit. Time: 2 days from Hayes River Guard Station.

MT. WILDER   5928

Located 1 mile north of the headwaters of Goldie River.

ROUTE. I, 2. From Happy Hollow Shelter (see Mt. Dana, Route 1), gain the crest of the main ridge joining Mt. Barnes and Mt. Dana. Follow the ridge NE ca. 1 mile on game trails to the small rounded top. Time: 4 hours from camp.

MT. BARNES   5993

Located on the north side of the head of Elwha Basin.

ROUTE 1. I, 2. Climb E from Dodwell-Rixon Pass 1 mile to the summit over easy rock and snow, or 1 mile SE from Bear Pass along the ridge crest. Time: 5 hours from Happy Hollow Shelter.

ROUTE 2. I, 2. From Happy Hollow Shelter (see Mt. Dana, Route 1) climb to the crest of the main ridge joining Mt. Barnes and Mt. Dana, coming out at a silver forest burn. Follow the ridge NW via a game trail 2½ miles to the summit. Time: 4 hours from camp.

For a different route down, follow a spur ridge SW to the Elwha Snowfinger via elk trails which come out to the river opposite "The Big Snow Hump" bypassing Dodwell-Rixon Pass.

MT. QUEETS   6480

Located between the Queets and Elwha Basins.

First ascent 1907 by A. Curtis, G. Humes, and W. Price.

ROUTE 1. II, 2. From the end of the maintained Elwha River trail, 2½ miles above Happy Hollow Shelter, cross the river, traveling up the grassy Elwha Basin along the right (NE) bank of an unnamed stream that runs off Mt. Queets. Proceed up a snowfield above a waterfall for an additional ½ mile. A marked way trail leads over a rocky knob above this snowfield to an open gully leading to the right into the timber. Follow the markers on a traverse through big trees for ½ mile, then drop to the Elwha Snowfinger. In some seasons the Elwha River can be followed direct, on the right side, to this point, but it may take more time than the route described above.

Continue up the Snowfinger to "The Big Snow Hump," a characteristic bulge caused by snow movement off Mt. Queets and Mt. Barnes. At this hump, turn left and follow an open chute over snow, scree, and polished rock to an upper bowl. By climbing left to the rim, gain the summit snowfield and follow it to the main ridge crest. The highest point, the middle squarish rock protruding from the upper rim, is reached by crossing a moat, followed by a short rock scramble. Time: 4 hours from Happy Hollow Shelter.

ROUTE 2. II, 2. From Elwha Basin (see Route 1 above), cross the unnamed stream and travel SW into Noyes Basin between Mt. Seattle, Mt. Noyes, Mt. Meany, and Mt. Queets. Ascend creek and snowfield ½ mile to a gully leading up to the snowfield at the E base of Mt. Meany. Follow the narrow ridge crest at the top of the snowfield which joins Mt. Meany and Mt. Queets. Ascend the summit snowfield of Mt. Queets to the moat of Route 1. Time: 5 hours from Elwha Basin.

MT. MEANY   6695

Located between Mt. Queets and Mt. Noyes.

First ascent 1907 by A. Curtis, L. Nelson, and P. McGregor.

ROUTE. II, 3. From Elwha Basin, cross to the Noyes Basin (see Route 2, Mt. Queets) and ascend a gully leading to an upper bench and snowfield at the E base of Mt. Meany. Climb the snowfield to the summit block where a narrow chimney and ledge lead to the broken-up top. The rock climbing is not as difficult as it first appears. Time: 4 hours from Elwha Basin.

The narrow ridge and snowfield have been traversed from Mt. Queets (see also Mt. Queets, Routes 1 and 2).

References: 1923 *Trail and Timberline;* 1907–08, 1913, 1920, and 1926 *Mountaineer;* 1926 and 1928 *Mazama.*

MT. NOYES   ca. 6100

Located between Mt. Meany and Mt. Seattle.

First ascent 1907 by A. Curtis and G. Humes.

ROUTE 1. II, 2. Take the Skyline trail from the Low Divide, through Seattle Creek Basin to where the trail switchbacks down to the W (ca. 3 miles). Climb N to the notch in the ridge between Mt. Noyes and Mt. Seattle. Ascend a rotten ridge left to the summit. Time: 4 hours from Low Divide.

ROUTE 2. II, 2. From Elwha Basin, climb S through Noyes Basin to the notch between Mt. Seattle and Mt. Noyes. Continue up the righthand ridge to the summit. Time: 3 hours.

ROUTE 2-V. II, 2. An easier approach is to turn right from well up the Noyes snowfield to a notch between Mt. Noyes and Mt. Meany. Climb left up the N ridge of Mt. Noyes. A rock scramble leads to the summit. Time: 3 hours from Elwha Basin.

The rock pinnacle on the ridge between Mt. Seattle and Mt.

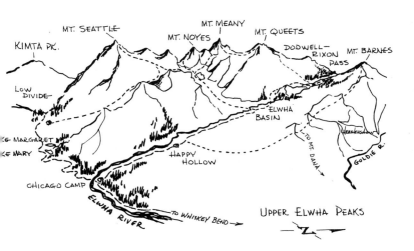

UPPER ELWHA PEAKS

Noyes is *Cougar Mountain* and involves a Class 3 rock scramble
from either side or by either end.

MT. SEATTLE   6246

Located on the south side of Elwha Basin, 1½ miles west of
Low Divide.

First ascent 1907 by A. Curtis, G. Humes, and L. Nelson.

ROUTE 1. I, 2. From Elwha Basin, cross left into Noyes
Basin. Gain the notch on the N ridge of Mt. Seattle via a
brushy gully and snowfields. From the ridge, go around the E
side of the first peak to the SE peak which is the highest. Time:
5 hours from Elwha Basin.

ROUTE 2. I, 2. For this by no means new, but previously
unlisted route, follow the National Park waterline service trail
from the Low Divide Patrol Cabin to the dam. Cross to the
right (E) side of the creek, working up a ridge via elk trails and
markers a distance of ½ mile where the trail breaks out of timber. Traverse to meadows above a waterfall. From here, follow
systems of snowfields and rock benches to the saddle between
the main peaks. The peak on the left (S) is slightly higher. Time:
4 hours from Low Divide. The summit can also be reached via
the Seattle Creek Basin, either up the S ridge or by the Mt.
Noyes-Mt. Seattle ridge.

References: 1907–08, 1920, and 1926 *Mountaineer*.

MT. CHRISTIE   6179

Located 2 miles southeast of Low Divide.

First ascent 1907 by A. Curtis and party.

ROUTE 1. II, 3. Take the way trail from Lake Margaret
through Martin Park to the head of the cirque where the trail
doubles back to the left to Martin Lakes. Cross the cirque and
ascend the glacier on the NE side of the peak to the ridge crest.
Follow this ridge westerly around the head of the Christie Glacier, which flows W to the North Fork Quinault River drainage.
The highest point is on the SW side of the massif. Time: 5 hours
from Low Divide.

ROUTE 2. II, 3. From two-thirds of the way up the glacier
out of the cirque (see Route 1 above), turn right up a shallow

gully to a saddle on the right of "Bottle Butte." This flat saddle has a USGS monument, with an arrow pointing to the summit across the Christie Glacier. Drop 75 ft. through a snowfinger notch to the large Christie Glacier. Cross the glacier on a near-level traverse to a notch in the final ridge slightly left of the summit. Time: 4 hours from Low Divide.

ROUTE 3. II, 3. From the lower end of Martin Park (ca. 1 mile from Lake Margaret), ascend the first snow gully on the right to gain the ridge separating Martin Park from the Christie Glacier. Cross the ridge and descend elk trails to the glacier via any one of several routes. Ascend the glacier to gain the final notch of Route 2 above. Time: 3½ hours from Low Divide.

KIMTA PEAK   5399

Located on the Queets-North Fork Quinault River divide at the head of Kimta Creek.

ROUTE. I, 1. The summit is just off the Skyline trail 11 miles from Low Divide, or 16 miles from North Fork Quinault Campground.

MT. ZINDORF   5539

This large massif, prominently seen 4 miles to the southwest from Low Divide, is located between Promise Creek and the North Fork Quinault River. It was named by the Press Party Expedition.

ROUTE. I, 2. Leave the Skyline trail at the head of Promise Creek 2 miles E of Kimta Peak. Follow the easy ridge E just less than 2 miles to the summit. The second of two peaks is the highest. Time: 7 hours from Low Divide.

MT. LAWSON   5401

Located on a spur between Geoduck Creek and Rustler Creek, halfway between Francis Creek Shelter and Twelve Mile Shelter.

ROUTE. I, 2. From ½ mile S of Geoduck Creek, cross the North Fork Quinault River and climb SE to parallel the N ridge. Gain the easy ridge and follow it S to the summit. Distance is 3 miles from Twelve Mile Shelter. Time: 3 hours.

HIGH ALPINE TRAVERSES

The traverses described in this section are a form of wilderness travel which is a cross between hiking and climbing. Many of them can be used as approaches to climbs, but they are being recommended for scenery and interest as well as for mountaineering experiences in their own right. Travel is off the trails, mostly in high open meadow, scree, snow, and rock. Some brush is encountered, but this is the exception. Routefinding and map-reading skills are necessary for these traverses. Moderate rock-scrambling ability will suffice. Snow in excess of 30° will be found on some routes, and an ice axe should be carried. Two of the routes, Queets Basin to Glacier Meadows and Hayden Pass to Anderson Pass, cross living glaciers and require full crevasse-rescue skill and equipment.

All route descriptions are based on the 15-minute USGS quadrangle maps. The sheet needed is listed in each traverse. Even with a map, guide book, compass, and altimeter, routefinding ability will still be needed. Anyone in doubt about his skill and experience should start on the shorter and easier routes before trying more extended trips.

Weather is the main hazard for alpine travel in the Olympics. Along these traverses, even hikers knowing the route can become confused in fog, rain, or snow, and be forced to wait out the weather. This possibility should be considered when planning time and equipment for a trip. Some emergency equipment should always be taken for even short trips above timberline.

At the High Divide (Roy Etten)

See the section on mountain safety for more information on this subject.

The time required for these trips will vary greatly depending on conditioning, experience, knowledge of the route, and whims of the hiker. Times for very strong and experienced hikers are included in the description to give some idea of what is possible.

BAILEY RANGE

Through the use of this cross-country route plus the trail from Low Divide to the Quinault River via the ridge between the Queets and Quinault (Skyline trail), it is possible to cross the Olympics from north to south entirely in high, scenic country. The route is described in sections, but it can be done in one grand traverse, or a few sections at a time. Some segments offer enjoyment as day trips for strong hikers.

This traverse is the classic "Crisler Route" made popular by Herb Crisler, who photographed the Disney film *Olympic Elk* in the Bailey Range in the 1930s and early 1940s. The route was first traveled by Billy Everett, who reached Cream Lake Basin in 1885 at the age of 16. Billy made the traverse many times, and may have been the first man to climb Mt. Carrie, Mt. Fitzhenry, and others.

Before the trails were built, travel along the high ridges was easier in many places than crashing up the brushy river valleys. Some of these high routes were followed more often years ago by hunters, trappers, prospectors, and "mountain men" than they are today.

All sections of the Bailey Range traverse are covered on the 15-minute USGS Mt. Olympus quadrangle, and the references to names and elevations are from that map.

Boulder Lake to Appleton Pass

This entire route is scenic and alpine, with less than 5 miles of off-trail travel. Since both ends of the route join trails from Olympic Hot Springs, this makes an excellent loop hike of 2

days, or it can be done in a single day from the road by strong
hikers.

From Boulder Lake, 3½ miles by trail from Olympic Hot
Springs, the route is southerly to Lower Three Horse Lake,
using a contour at or below 4500 feet. Game trails may be followed. Continue up the drainage above Lower Three Horse
Lake for ½ mile to a small creek from the S which drains a
basin W of Everett Peak. Hike up into this basin, staying E of
the creek on game trails. From the pass in the ridge joining Everett Peak with the main ridge, descend SE through meadows to
Blue Lake. From here, the route is S again, on the flat ridge just
E of Blue Lake. Follow this ridge S into another basin where
scenic Mud Lake lies under the N face of Mt. Appleton. This
pool was omitted from the 1956 USGS Mt. Olympus quadrangle. From Mud Lake, climb SW up a permanent 30° snowfield
to a notch separating the basin from the Soleduck drainage. Descend scree to the large basins of a tributary of the North Fork
Soleduck River. Hold to the upper basin and traverse S to reach
the ridge separating this drainage from the main Soleduck
River drainage. This ridge should be gained at about 5500 feet.
Next, contour the S side of the 6100-foot summit located NW
of Appleton Pass, reaching the Appleton Pass trail one or two
switchbacks S of the pass. This unnamed 6100-foot summit,
higher than Mt. Appleton, is located on the main ridge and thus
is frequently confused with Mt. Appleton, which is ½ mile to
the N.

Appleton Pass to Cat Basin

The traverse from Appleton Pass to Cat Basin provides about 5
miles of off-trail travel, and is an easy one-day trip. It can be
done from the road by strong hikers in a long day, returning to
either Olympic Hot Springs via the Appleton Pass trail or to Sol
Duc Hot Springs via the Soleduck River trail. The total journey
involves 15 to 18 miles of trail travel in addition to the traverse.

Appleton Pass is reached via a 5-mile trail from Olympic Hot
Springs. From the pass, go E and S in scenic alpland along the
ridge separating the Soleduck River from Boulder and Schoeffel

Creeks. In about 2 miles this ridge intersects the ridge bounding Cat Creek on the W at a summit which is avoided by a sidehill traverse on elk trails. The last ½ mile is on the Soleduck side. Traverse to a notch where small ponds can be seen in the Cat Creek drainage. Continue S from this notch in cirques on the Cat Creek side of the ridge, staying above 5000 feet, just under the last upper cliffs on the ridge crest. The last cirque can be located on the map by looking across the ridge SE of Haigs Lake. From the last cirque, ascend to the brushy ridge bounding it on the S to overlook the extensive meadows of upper Cat Basin and the High Divide. Descend through brush to Cat Basin. From the large basin, an old trail to a CCC trail camp leads up to High Divide, or any of several elk trails may be followed to the end of the traverse at the divide.

Cat Basin to Mt. Ferry

Though the distance is less than 10 miles, a full day should be allowed for this section, since routefinding between Mt. Carrie and Cream Lake Basin can slow the pace. An early start is advised, for campsites are infrequent and marginal between "Boston Charlie's Camp" and Cream Lake. In addition to the following alpine route, the range can be traversed across the summits of the peaks from the top of Mt. Carrie (see Climbing Routes, page 141).

High Divide, above Cat Basin or Heart Lake, is reached by 8 to 10 miles of trail from Sol Duc Hot Springs. An unfinished CCC trail continues SE to a dead-end in rock cliffs between Cat Peak and Mt. Carrie. From the trail end, climb a few hundred feet to the ridge crest, a narrow, steep, brushy arête known as the "Cat Walk," which is less difficult than it appears. Continue SE along the "Cat Walk," either on the crest or a few feet down the N side, allowing an hour to traverse this arête.

Just across the "Cat Walk" is a small pond and "Boston Charlie's Camp." Named for an early "mountain man," this is one of the few campsites with water on this section of the traverse. From "Boston Charlie's," the route gains several hundred feet in elevation and traverses the grassy S shoulder of Mt. Carrie. Continue SE to the Cream Lake area along the SW side of the Bailey Range at the 5000 to 5500-ft. level, making use of slight game trails. The main difficulties are the many gullies to be crossed and the traverse of steep grass and scree. Avoid going too low, for large gullies draining into the Hoh River can create difficulties.

Once the spur ridge SW of Peak 5978 is reached, the terrain lessens in difficulty, and a variety of routes can be taken. If Cream Lake is the goal, descend. If you elect to continue to Mt. Ferry, stay high past Cream Lake. The area to the W of Mt. Ferry is open, travel is easy, campsites abound, and several lakelets dot the landscape.

From Mt. Ferry Basin, there are three possible routes to the crest of the Bailey Range. The summit can be traversed, and though not difficult, this entails the most work. The valley between Mt. Ferry and Peak 6283 (Pulitzer or Snagtooth) is easy to ascend past the remnant glacier. The heather meadows S of Pulitzer are also easy, leading up to the crest of the range at a flat area S of this peak. Once on top, travel is simple to the E of both Pulitzer and Ferry on broad, grassy benches. From the Ferry plateau, routes continue to either Queets Basin or Dodger Point.

Mt. Ferry to Dodger Point

Distance for this easy section is about 4 miles, and it can be traveled in ½ day or less. This is a good route to use either as a retreat from the Bailey Range, or to divide the Bailey Range traverse into smaller sections. Dodger Point is 13 miles from the road (Whiskey Bend) via the Long Ridge trail.

From the broad bench E of the summit of Mt. Ferry, descend the ridge E to the saddle at the headwaters of Long Creek. The descent is not difficult, but has one short, steep place. Continue NE in open meadows on the divide between Long Creek and the Goldie River. From this ridge, two routes are possible. One involves climbing over the summit of Ludden Peak and then descending steep cliff bands to the E to gain the trail to Dodger

Point. A more moderate route is via open slopes to the flat meadow that lies between Ludden Peak and Mt. Scott, descending just W of Ludden's summit. From the Ludden-Scott saddle, which provides an excellent campsite, descend NE for a few hundred feet, then continue just under the rock cliffs that form the SE side of Ludden Peak. Look up NE for a trail partially blasted out of rock. Ascend at the first opportunity to the unfinished trail, and follow it to the Dodger Point trail. This old trail, seldom shown on maps, stretches along the E side of Ludden Peak to within ½ mile of the Ludden-Scott saddle.

Mt. Ferry to Queets Basin

This section covers about 6 miles and is an easy day in good conditions. However, like most of the Bailey Range, it is very exposed to storms and fog.

From the flat ridgetop S of Mt. Ferry and Mt. Pulitzer (Snagtooth), ascend a snow slope and continue S down the crest of the Bailey Range over easy summits and along ridges. Cut across the top of a snowfield shown on the map just N of Peak 6205 (Mt. Childs). From the snowfield, cross the ridge to the E side of the crest of the range, and pick up broad benches E of Mt. Childs. Follow these benches S to Bear Pass. Bear Pass is a broad shoulder W of Peak 5819, not a true pass. From Bear Pass, open slopes of meadow or snow lead SW down to the vast Queets Basin with its lakelet and numerous campsites.

Queets Basin to Elwha Basin

This cross-country route ends at the terminus of the Elwha River trail in a meadow at the confluence of the Elwha River and the creek draining Mt. Noyes. This location is marked as Elwha Basin on the USGS Mt. Olympus quadrangle. Elwha Basin is 30 miles by trail from the Elwha River road end at Whiskey Bend, and 22 miles by trail from the end of the North Fork Quinault River road and via Low Divide. The route through upper Queets Basin over Dodwell-Rixon Pass and down the Elwha Snowfinger to Elwha Basin is about 4 miles with a 2000-ft. loss in elevation. The descent will take several hours. This is a good route for access to or retreat from the high country, and a good way of ending the traverse. It is also a natural link with the trails or routes out of Low Divide.

Dodwell-Rixon Pass is located in a somewhat hidden notch in the SE corner of upper Queets Basin. This natural approach to the high country was one of the first used by explorers, surveyors, and mountaineers. The position of the pass should be determined and a compass bearing noted before traveling the area, in case of poor visibility enroute. From Dodwell-Rixon Pass, the moderate Elwha Snowfinger descends SE to the upper Elwha River. This is not a glacier, but it can be large and may last all year. Avalanches from Mt. Queets, Mt. Meany, Mt. Barnes, and Mt. Noyes pour tons of snow and debris onto the Elwha Snowfinger each year, mostly in winter and spring. Hazards of moats and melt holes exist especially where streams run under the snow. Descend the snowfinger and cross to the SW side of the river at ca. 3200 feet. A faintly marked way trail leads up a steep, brushy slope above where the river drops into a gorge. The trail traverses a wet bench and crosses a ridge at 3400 feet, then emerges into the open meadows of Elwha Basin next to an unnamed and unmapped stream and waterfalls from the E face of Mt. Queets. The Elwha River must again be crossed to reach the upper end of the Elwha River trail. There are good campsites in the basin, or 2½ miles downtrail at Happy Hollow Camp.

Queets Basin to Glacier Meadows

This route, across the NE side of Mt. Olympus, crosses three major glaciers and requires mountaineering skill, roped travel, and crevasse-rescue knowledge and equipment. Allow at least a full day for this traverse. For additional details on the area, see Climbing Routes, page 124. Glacier Meadows is 18 miles by trail from the end of the Hoh River road.

From Queets Basin, cross the river and ascend to the W, gaining the Humes Glacier via the rocks on its S side above the terminal ice cliffs. Ascend the glacier to Blizzard Pass, which separates the Humes and Hoh Glaciers. From Blizzard Pass, descend steep snow and ice to the Hoh Glacier. Difficulty on the Hoh

Glacier will depend on the time of year, and may vary from one year to the next. Cross the Hoh Glacier to the W, and climb to Glacier Pass (marked "Blizzard Pass" on the 1956 USGS Mt. Olympus quadrangle), which is S of Peak 7168 (Mt. Mathias). From Glacier Pass descend the Blue Glacier on moderate slopes. The route off the Blue Glacier is on the NE side near the snout, where a trail leads to Glacier Meadows. An old trail also follows the top of the lateral moraine E of the Blue Glacier for the last ½ mile, but it may be difficult to gain the crest in some seasons.

DUNGENESS-DOSEWALLIPS AREA

The ranges of the northeast Olympics do not lie in one long chain to form a single traverse as does the Bailey Range to the west. However, some of the routes do link up to form longer trips. Three of the four routes can be done in 2 days or less, and offer good trips for the weekender. Most can be worked out to end at the same point as the start, to simplify transportation. All are outstanding mountaineering ventures.

Gray Wolf Ridge to Royal Basin
(USGS Tyler Peak Quadrangle)

This trip has been done in 1 long day from the road, returning by trail from Royal Basin. Distance is about 8 miles off trail, and 6 miles by trail from Royal Basin to the road.

The Dungeness River road in Olympic National Forest (road #295) extends almost to Royal Creek, then switches back and climbs to the NW (see Dungeness River approach in Climbing Routes, page 86). About ½ mile NW of the switchback, look for a steep, unmarked cat track leading NW up the ridge. This fire trail follows the general line of the old Maynard Burn waytrail. Take the fire trail to ca. 5000 feet, where it ends at the National Park boundary, and continue on the old waytrail to timberline. Ascend through easy, open terrain to the summit of Baldy. This summit can also be reached via an abandoned lookout trail which climbs to timberline from Slide Camp on the Gray Wolf River trail.

From Baldy, traverse S at the 6000- to 7000-ft. level in meadow, scree, or snow, all the way to The Needles. Stay on the ridge crest most of the way. Peak 7076 can be climbed by way of a basin between the double summit to avoid a broken ridge. Once past Peak 7076, the next summit is in The Needles, and requires technical climbing. To continue to Royal Basin, descend SE over steep broken slopes and chutes to the Royal Basin trail below the basin.

A recommended alternate route from the ridgetop is to work W around Peak 7378 (Mt. Walkinshaw) by way of a basin N of the peak, then climb to the NW ridge of Mt. Walkinshaw at ca. 6750 feet. From here, drop to the valley W of The Needles. Continue up this valley, which leads into Surprise Pass just SW of Peak 7528 (Mt. Clark). The climb to the pass is up steep snow or ice, requiring mountaineering skill and equipment. From Surprise Pass, drop into open, snowy Surprise Basin, and continue on easy terrain for 1 mile to Royal Lake.

Royal Basin to Constance Pass
(USGS Tyler Peak Quadrangle)

This traverse can be done in a day by a strong hiker coming out the Dosewallips, but 2 or more days are recommended. Distance off trails is about 8 miles.

From Royal Lake (7 miles by trail from the Dungeness River road), hike S up the valley. The brushy headwall just above the lake is the only difficult terrain in the open, scenic valley. At the head of the valley, ascend to the divide E of the remnant glacier on the NE side of Mt. Deception. From this ridge, descend open slopes to the basin at the head of Deception Creek. Continue downstream from Deception Basin to the valley leading SE to the notch between Mt. Mystery and Little Mystery. Ascend scree or snow to this notch (Gunsight Pass).

An alternate route leads from Deception Basin to the Dosewallips River trail near Deception Creek. This route stays just out of the canyon of Deception Creek on the NW side.

From Gunsight Pass, traverse E to gain the ridge between the Dosewallips and Dungeness drainages, and follow it to a point where you can drop into Sunny Brook Meadows and the Constance Pass trail. The section between Peak 6666 and Peak 6576 is broken, and is best avoided by dropping to the meadows even if you are continuing E to Constance Pass. You can return to the Dungeness River road via Home Lake and the Dungeness River trail, or descend the Constance Pass trail to the Dosewallips River trail and road.

Grand Valley to Lost Basin via Lake Lillian
(USGS Mt. Angeles Quadrangle)

This trip from Obstruction Point and the return by trail has been completed in one day by strong hikers, but 2 days are recommended. The distance off trail is about 6 miles.

There is a low, unnamed pass at the head of Grand Valley just above the point where the trail turns SE toward Grand Pass. Leave the trail at the turn (5 miles from the end of the Obstruction Point road) and ascend SW to this broad, unnamed pass. Ignore traces of an abandoned trail, for it leads into the tangled avalanche debris of 1949. Instead, continue into the Lillian drainage to the flat meadows at the base of McCartney Peak, through brush in places. Follow the meadows westerly around the N side of the peak to the creek draining Lake Lillian, where the abandoned trail can be regained and ascended on the E side of the stream to the open basins at the lake. Meadow, scree, or snow lead to the pass above Lake Lillian. Cross the pass into the Lost River drainage and regain the abandoned trail, following it SE below the ridge crest toward Lost Basin. Climb to the ridge crest at Peak 6443, and bypass Peak 6733 a few hundred feet below the summit on the SW slope. The route joins the Cameron Creek-to-Dose Meadows trail in Lost Basin a few hundred yards S of Cameron Pass. From Cameron Pass, the Dosewallips River road can be reached in 16 miles via Lost Pass and the Dosewallips River trail, or Obstruction Point can be reached in 12 miles via Grand Pass.

Hayden Pass to Anderson Pass
(USGS Mt. Angeles and Mt. Steel Quadrangles)

This rather difficult route involves the ascent and descent of two glaciers, and should only be attempted by experienced parties equipped for crevasse rescue. Though the 6-mile distance is frequently done in 1 day, most parties prefer to establish a camp in the alpine meadow near the snout of the Eel Glacier.

From Hayden Pass (15 miles by trail from the Dosewallips River road and 25 miles from Whiskey Bend on the Elwha River road), go S around Sentinel Peak on the W side of the ridge. Contour southerly, bypassing Peak 6301 to the E. Continue S on game trails and meadows, staying high to avoid the brushy cliffs and waterfalls of the Silt Creek canyon. After about 1½ miles, drop gradually to Silt Creek, to where it is a flat outwash from the terminus of the Eel Glacier.

Eel Glacier is moderate, but presents crevasse hazard. Climb to the obvious notch (Flypaper Pass) at the head of the glacier W of the summit of Mt. Anderson. A steep snow chute descends S to the moderate Anderson Glacier from the pass. Descend Anderson Glacier, leaving it at its southeastern edge to pass E of a small terminal lake, and climb a moraine SE to a small pond and campsites in meadows. This pond appears on the Mt. Steel quadrangle in the upper drainage of the West Fork Dosewallips River. A good trail leads from the meadow to Anderson Pass. A direct route to the Quinault drainage from the Anderson Glacier should not be attempted, as it involves severe cliffs.

SKOKOMISH-HAMMA HAMMA AREA

Gladys Divide, located above Flapjack Lakes, is 6 miles by trail from the end of the Skokomish River road in the Staircase area of Olympic National Park. From Gladys Divide, a traverse in very interesting alpine country can be made to First Divide and the Skokomish River trail. It is 9 miles by this trail to the same road end where the traverse started.

A waytrail from a logging road on the Hamma Hamma River can be used to enter the traverse in the middle near Lake of the

Hart Lake, in La Crosse Basin, near the Head of the Duckabush River (George W. Martin)

Angels (see approach to Mt. Stone, Climbing Routes, page 45, for this route). The trail to Upper Lena Lake (6 miles by trail from the Hamma Hamma River road) can also be used as a starting or ending point for a traverse in this area. All the traverses described here are located on the USGS Mt. Steel and The Brothers quadrangles.

Total distance for the entire trip to First Divide and return is 15 miles on trail and at least 8 miles cross country. The traverse has been done in a single day, but most parties should plan at least 2 days.

Gladys Divide to Lake of the Angels

This trip can be done in 1 day from the Skokomish River road. Distance is 6 miles by trail and about 4 miles off trail.

At Gladys Divide, descend NE into the Hamma Hamma River drainage to an obvious flat avalanche meadow. It is difficult to contour across without losing elevation due to gullies and slide alder. A direct traverse over Mt. Henderson and Mt. Skokomish is long, and involves climbing problems. From the meadow at about 4000 feet, climb NE up a draw to notches in the ridge extending S from Mt. Skokomish. Cross one of the notches to the cirque on the E side. Stay high here and cross the ridge N of this cirque to the next basin which is the source of Whitehorse Creek. The lake shown on the map is Lake of the Angels.

Lake of the Angels to First Divide

This pleasant traverse in alpland is about 6 miles, and can be done in a short day.

From the small lake at the head of Whitehorse Creek (Lake of the Angels), climb a few hundred feet NW to the pass above. From this pass, descend the headwall to the basin at the source of the Skokomish River. Climb N on scree and heather or snow to a saddle just W of Mt. Stone, which is located exactly on the National Park boundary and the county line. This saddle has been known as "The Great Stone Arrow" due to rock markings in heather.

It is easy to walk down to Hagen Lake from this pass, then contour WNW in heather and fir to the basin at the head of Crazy Creek. An easy ascent can then be made from the basin to the ridge crest SE of Mt. Hopper. This point can also be reached directly from "The Great Stone Arrow" by following the ridge NW. A waytrail leads from this point to the Skokomish River trail at First Divide, which is 9 miles by trail from the Skokomish River road.

Upper Lena Lake to Lake of the Angels

This pleasant traverse, largely in alpland, is about 5 miles and can be completed in a short day.

From Upper Lena Lake, 6 miles by trail from the Hamma Hamma River road, follow waytrails westerly to the ridge S of Mt. Lena. Continue through the pass approximately 1½ miles SW of Scout Lake to the two lakes on the fork of Boulder Creek E of Mt. Stone. Pass the upper lake and climb SW to a 5900-ft. pass which separates the Boulder and Whitehorse Creek drainages. Moderate snow and scree lead to this pass in the SE ridge of Mt. Stone. Descend and work slightly W to Lake of the Angels at the source of Whitehorse Creek. Lake of the Angels, in open heather, can also be reached via a waytrail from the Hamma Hamma River road described in the approaches to Mt. Stone in Climbing Routes, page 45.

SKI AND SNOWSHOE TOURS

This section contains brief route descriptions of the better snow tours available in the Olympic Range. The best season for these is typically December through April or May.

Much of the Olympic Range is not ideal for oversnow travel. The snowline is variable and often quite high in elevation. Steep and heavily-timbered slopes extend far up most peaks, and upper basins are mostly deep within the range. Many of the high ridges are steep and therefore difficult to travel along for extended distances. Winter weather is a prime consideration with its potential for severe storm and avalanche. Despite possible difficulties and hazards, however, there are some very fine tours, and frequent periods of good weather and snow conditions.

Proper timing is extremely important for maximum success and safety on these tours. Both weather and snow conditions must be good. Be clothed and otherwise prepared for winter conditions, but pack light enough for reasonably fast travel. It is recommended that an ice axe be carried on most of these tours.

Moderate temperatures and steep slopes generally combine to make avalanche hazard in the Olympics more predictable than in colder ranges. Most avalanches occur during or soon after storms, and during sudden or extreme warming periods. High wind with drifting snow can also be dangerous. After a few days of good weather, the snow usually compacts, and skiing is possible again in the former avalanche area.

Snowshoeing on Copper Mountain (Glenn Kelsey)

As in all mountaineering ventures, it is wise to start with easy trips and work up to longer and more difficult ones as knowledge, skill, and strength increase. Most Olympic tours cover steep terrain where snowshoeing and even skiing is quite difficult. Few trips offer sustained downhill skiing. For these reasons, equipment is best chosen for traversing steep slopes, not for "schussing." Most of the trips described here have been done on wood Nordic touring skis.

Many of the following tours are approached via secondary or logging roads which are neither patrolled nor plowed in winter. Depending on the elevation of the snowline, upper portions of these roads may be impassable to automobiles for extended periods. In most cases the added distance of a road slog does not put the tour objective entirely out of reach; however, those who wish to avoid the extra oversnow travel should make local inquiry about road conditions before embarking on a particular trip. Remember also that a sudden snowstorm can trap a car until spring.

Hurricane Ridge Area

Several good tours start from this area, which is exceptionally scenic during good weather conditions. Owing to easy access, this is an excellent area to try out equipment and to get the feel of winter travel in these mountains.

A good paved road leaves U.S. 101 at Port Angeles and climbs south 17 miles to 5000-ft. Hurricane Ridge. This is the only place in the Olympics where a road is maintained into the alpine zone in winter. A day lodge and a small ski area are located here. Weather permitting, the road is open during the day each weekend during the winter season. On week days it is open only when the weather is good and no extra plowing is required. Blizzard conditions occasionally force closure of the road on scheduled open days.

Cars can be left overnight on the ridge only after checking with rangers, who will ensure that they are parked in a place safe from night snow-plow operations. The road closes each night, so register in person with rangers for any trip requiring a late return. Use the self-register at the lodge for short trips.

Recommended maps include the 15-minute Mt. Olympus and Mt. Angeles USGS quadrangles.

Hurricane Hill

This short and enjoyable tour is an excellent way to start Olympic touring. Distance from the parking lot to the summit is about 3 miles, with an elevation gain of about 1000 ft. Under good conditions this is an easy half-day trip.

Start at the W end of the parking lot and follow the snow covered road for about 1½ miles. The last 1½ miles are via trail along the S side of the ridge. When the snow is stable, an alternate route can be taken through the scenic valley N of the ridge for the last mile. Avoid cornices hanging off the N side of the ridge. Although there is some modest downhill skiing on return from the summit, this tour is mostly a ridge traverse.

Hurricane Ridge to Deer Park via Obstruction Point

This rewarding trip, primarily an above-timberline ridge run, has been done in a single day by strong skiers, but 2 days are recommended. The basic trip to Obstruction Point and return can be done in a full day. It is 9 miles to Obstruction Point, 8 miles farther along the ridge to Deer Park, and an additional 3 to 9 miles down the Deer Park road to the snow line. This route is very exposed to storms.

An unplowed road leaves the E end of the Hurricane Ridge parking area and continues along the ridge easterly for about 9 miles to Obstruction Point. To avoid bad sidehill at the start, leave the plowed main road about ½ mile below the parking lot. Drop down a moderate meadow slope to the Obstruction Point road. Portions of this road are hard to follow in deep drifts. The first 4 miles are moderate to easy in subalpine trees. The ridge then climbs 1000 ft. in elevation to Eagle Point. From Eagle Point to Obstruction Point, the route follows tundra-like meadow at about 6000 ft. Except for a little ankle-tiring sidehill, this section is moderately easy. Under most conditions, avalanche hazard is minimal if you stay on the S slopes.

At Obstruction Point, further progress is blocked by the steep narrow feature that gave the place its name. Passage past this point to Deer Park is recommended only under stable snow conditions. The route of the trail can be followed, but it traverses very steep sidehill under large cornices. The route directly over the top is relatively safe from avalanche, but is exposed and steep.

The first 3 miles past Obstruction Point lie along Elk Mountain. This is windswept tundra which is usually free from snow. This unusual alpine area is the location of a number of plants that grow only in this area, some blooming only in winter and early spring.

The road down from Deer Park is not plowed, and is usually snow covered for at least the upper 3 miles. Some years the entire 9 miles above the Park boundary is snowcovered, so local inquiry is advised. The road down can be an enjoyable ski run under good conditions.

Mt. Angeles

This pleasant peak provides an enjoyable ski mountaineering objective. Under good conditions it is a moderate day trip; either of two good approaches can be used.

For a touring approach, follow the ridge NE from the lodge for about 3 miles to the base of the peak.

If the chief objective is the peak, park the car at a small parking area about 9 miles above the National Park boundary (3½ miles down from the Hurricane Ridge parking area). Walk up the road about ½ mile and then climb up to the ridge crest at a low point S of the peak. This, known as Mt. Angeles saddle, is where the two approaches join. From the saddle, ascend northerly, keeping on the W side of the peak until just below the summit. Leave the skis here, and climb gully systems to the top.

The total elevation gain using the lower approach is 2000 ft. Of this, about 1600 ft. is good downhill skiing.

QUILCENE AREA

Lying in the rain shadow of the Olympics, this area offers some of the best weather in the range. In recent years both of the following tours have become increasingly popular. Both trips offer considerable downhill skiing on the return, a fairly uncommon situation in Olympic touring. Since the snow pack in the northeastern Olympics is relatively light, road approaches are more likely to be open here than in other areas. However, road conditions are variable and local inquiry should be made. The area is particularly well-suited to late winter and early spring trips.

Recommended maps are the 15-minute Tyler Peak and Quilcene USGS quadrangles for topography, and the most recent Olympic National Forest map for road approaches.

Mt. Townsend

This peak offers several scenic trips for the snowshoer as well as a variety of skiing including a number of alpine bowls. The lower slopes of this peak are laced to about 4000 ft. with logging roads which provide access for the various tours. While the following is recommended as a good day trip, other possibilities should not be ruled out. See Climbing Routes, page 107, for some of the other routes.

From Quilcene, take U.S. 101 N for about 2 miles. Turn W onto Forest Service road #2909 for 7 miles to a junction with road #2812. Follow road #2812 for 2¼ miles to where the Little Quilcene trail leaves for Mt. Townsend. Although a good snowshoe route, this trail is too narrow for good skiing, and for the skier it is best to continue on the road another mile past Little Quilcene River and some cliffs to an unmarked secondary logging road which branches right. Take this road about 1 mile to its end in a logged-off area. From the small creek at the upper end of this logged-off area, climb for 15 minutes along the right side of the creek to a small, flat, open area. Continue obliquely right, up a faint gully to the base of some cliffs, and then left through a narrow opening in the timber to an open flat area (approximately 30 minutes more). There is a saddle just above this flat and below a cliff. Climb to this saddle (4700 ft.) which offers a fine view of the skiing bowls above. Drop about 200 ft. into a basin which offers an excellent campsite. The shortest route to the summit leads through a small V-shaped group of trees directly to the top.

Marmot Pass-Mt. Buckhorn

This area of high open peaks and ridges offers very pleasant touring and ski mountaineering. Trail distance is 5 miles to Marmot Pass, and the trip can be done in a long day. However, 2 days, with a camp below Marmot Pass, is recommended.

Leave Forest Service road #272 at Tenmile shelter approximately 16 miles from U.S. 101 (see Climbing Routes, page 85, for details on this fairly complex approach). The trail follows the river for about 2½ miles through timber, to Shelter Rock Camp. It then climbs steeply for about 2½ miles to Marmot Pass. A spectacular view of the Ridge of Gargoyles is afforded along this section.

The slopes S of Marmot Pass toward Boulder Ridge and the bowl just E of the pass are the most challenging to skiers and hold snow the longest. Other possibilities from the pass are an easy ascent of Mt. Buckhorn or a traverse N over Buckhorn Pass to Copper City.

OLYMPIC HOT SPRINGS AREA

Olympic Hot Springs, located 18 miles southwest of Port Angeles at the end of the Elwha River-Olympic Hot Springs road, is the starting point of several interesting tours into the high country. The upper section of the road is not plowed, and the last 3 to 4 miles are usually under snow. However, the road is easy, sheltered by big timber, and pleasant to travel.

Required maps are the 15-minute Mt. Olympus and Joyce USGS quadrangles.

Boulder Lake

This trip begins in timber and gradually climbs into scenic, semi-open meadows. In case the road is snowed in for several miles below the campground, this is a fairly strenuous full-day trip. The trail distance is about 3½ miles.

From the Olympic Hot Springs Campground, follow the trail W for 1 mile to the trail fork. Follow the right fork, which goes to Boulder Lake. This trail climbs gradually in large timber to the upper basin containing the lake. Snow is usually heavy on the trail above the 2-mile point even in late spring, and this section is marked for winter travel. Snow is sometimes sparse below mile two. The upper basin is semi-open, and very scenic in winter. A steep section in heavy timber just below this basin is moderately difficult if icy. The run down is in timber, but not difficult unless the snow is icy.

Appleton Pass

This trip begins in heavy timber and climbs into a picturesque alpine setting at Appleton Pass. The trail distance is 5 miles. Two days are recommended when the road is snowed in. This trip is more difficult than Boulder Lake because there are several creek crossings, the route is not well marked, and it is higher and steeper.

Leave the campground and follow the trail W to the Boulder Lake-Appleton Pass junction. Continue along the main trail past the fork going to Boulder Lake. Two log crossings of Boulder Creek may provide problems. The upper crossing can sometimes be made about 300 yards above the log on avalanche snow that often bridges the creek. As the trail gains elevation, it becomes harder to follow in and out of meadows. The final ascent to the pass is best accomplished using the map, as all signs of the trail will be hidden under the snow. For the last portion to the ridge, follow the valley and then climb up near Oyster Lake. Skiing back down this route is good, and there will be a long alpine run under proper conditions. There are a few steep pitches and much moderate open skiing. This is recommended as a spring trip, when one can drive to the trailhead and walk up through the timbered section.

Happy Lake Ridge

This strenuous 2-day loop is rewarding for the well-conditioned. The route includes some very scenic stretches which provide views of the main Olympic peaks that are seldom seen in winter. While this tour can be accomplished from either direction, it is recommended to go in the Happy Lake trail and out via Boulder Lake, particularly if skiing. Distance is 3 miles to the ridge top, 7 miles along the ridge to Boulder Lake, and 3½ miles to the end of the Olympic Hot Springs road. Be prepared for an added 2 to 4 miles down the snowcovered road. This trip is much easier (1 full day) in early spring when the road is open to Olympic Hot Springs, and the trail is bare much of the way to the ridge crest.

The trail to Happy Lake Ridge leaves the Olympic Hot Springs road about 5 miles above the Elwha Ranger Station. Many winters, this is about as far as the road is open. Since the trail ascends the sunny side of the slope, the snowline is high compared to that of the sheltered road below. The trail is steep with much sidehill near the top.

After 3 miles the broad, timbered ridge crest is reached. Follow the ridge crest westerly to Happy Lake. The ridge is open near Happy Lake, but timbered and narrow in many other places. Past Happy Lake divide, take care to stay to the left. There is a tendency to go too far in an open meadow that leads to a dead-end spur ridge. Careful map reading will avoid this. Continue on to a point above Boulder Lake and then descend in semi-open meadows to the lake, where the trail can be picked up. It is advisable to know the route down from Boulder Lake before embarking on this tour. See the Boulder Lake tour for more information.

SEVEN LAKES BASIN LOOP

This very rewarding and scenic tour provides spectacular views of Mt. Olympus in good weather. The trip is not recommended for beginners and the route should be scouted in the summer first. Wait for good weather and stable snow before starting this loop. The best conditions in both the valley and the basin occur when the snowline is at about 3500 ft. This also allows driving to the trailhead and walking the lower part of the trail. Skis are recommended for this trip, because of extensive sidehill travel.

The time required will vary greatly depending on the party, weather, and snow conditions. Although the trip has been accomplished in 1 day, 2 or 3 days are recommended. The total distance is 20 miles, 10 miles through the high country and 10 miles through forest.

This loop trip starts and finishes at the end of the Soleduck River road (about 2 miles above Sol Duc Hot Springs). A mile up the trail at Soleduck Falls the trail forks. One branch is used as the start of the loop and the other for the return. The tour is practical from either direction, but the Deer Lake start is recommended since there is a chance of getting wet feet in the river crossings between Soleduck Falls and Soleduck Park.

It is 3 miles through timber to Deer Lake. The route from Deer Lake to the divide between the Soleduck and Bogachiel Rivers climbs through pleasant meadow country, with an elevation gain of 1000 ft. From this divide to the Seven Lakes Basin trail junction (ca. 2 miles) stay on the Bogachiel River side, following the trail route through the tree section. About a mile from the junction, the terrain becomes steep open sidehill which can be avoided by descending several hundred feet to slight benching. Continue S, climbing back up to the ridge trough (at the trail junction). Next, descend to Round Lake and Lunch Lake in the basin. The slope is steep at the top, but eases off below to provide a good ski run. Do not try to stay high around Bogachiel Peak, because the sidehill there is steep and dangerous.

The basin country is open and the deep snow rounds everything off, making the route E from Lunch Lake easy. Climb NE up a broad draw and hit High Divide at a low point (ca. 5000 ft.) directly above Morgenroth Lake as identified on the 15-minute

Mt. Tom USGS quadrangle (misnamed on the 7.5-minute Boga-chiel quadrangle). Travel is easy from there along High Divide to Heart Lake Basin. Heart Lake Basin is open, providing good skiing down to Soleduck Park and below. Cross the creek above the headwall leading down from Soleduck Park, just past the large avalanche track from the west. This is where the creek leaves the meadows and starts into a canyon. The route from the headwall to the main Soleduck River crossing is steep and in timber. Take care to stay on the right side of the creeks and the main river, because the crossings are difficult due to deep snow and open water. There is a footlog at this time (1970) where the trail crosses the main river. If this crossing is difficult, see if the avalanche path near Seven Mile Shelter has formed a snow bridge. From Seven Mile Shelter out, there are usually snow patches even in light snow years.

Required maps are the 15-minute Mt. Olympus, Mt. Tom, and Mt. Carrie USGS quadrangles.

OLYMPIC CROSSING VIA HAYDEN PASS

Cross-Olympic trips are seldom done in winter due to difficulty, distance, weather, and avalanche hazard. Of the possible cross-Olympic routes, Hayden Pass from the Elwha River to the Dose-wallips River (or reverse) is the best. This trip involves no river crossings, and there is usually a clean snowline on the southern-exposed ascent to the pass, with a good open snow descent on the Dosewallips side. At this time, there are also shelters along this route.

Total distance for this trip is 40 miles over trails alone, with probable added distance because of snowed-in roads. Snow conditions and snowlines vary greatly with time. The best time to make the trip is with the snowline at about 3000 ft. This provides open roads and allows walking up the low valleys. Under ideal conditions, this trip can be done in 3 days. The Dosewallips River road may be snowed in at times, so local inquiry should be made before the trip.

The trip starts (or finishes) at Whiskey Bend on the Elwha River. Skis or snowshoes may have to be packed up the Elwha

River to Hayes River or above (16 or more miles). The climb from Elwha River to Hayden Pass has a good grade, and the trail can usually be followed on snow to the start of the meadows (3 miles below the pass). From there, the pass must be located by landmarks alone, which is not difficult in good weather. Under most conditions, this traverse is safe from avalanche. From Hayden Pass, open slopes lead all the way down to the upper meadows of the Dosewallips River, affording an excellent ski run. A large cornice on Mt. Claywood towers over part of the route. The only avalanche release zone which must be crossed is near the top of the pass. Once in the vicinity of Dose Meadows there is little further avalanche hazard, and there is good skiing for a number of miles. The lower 9 miles of the Dosewallips River trail are in timber, and snow conditions vary greatly.

Required maps are the 15-minute Mt. Olympus, Mt. Angeles, and Tyler Peak USGS quadrangles.

STAIRCASE-SKOKOMISH AREA

The alpine meadows around and above Flapjack Lakes have long been enjoyed as a winter touring area. While the trail distance to the lakes is only 4.5 miles, the road above Staircase Ranger Station is often snowed in, and a minimum of 2 days is recommended for this trip in winter.

From Staircase Ranger Station (see Climbing Routes, page 35, for approach details), a dirt road climbs about 4 miles to the trailhead. During winters of heavy snowfall this road is snowed in; however, it is enjoyable Nordic skiing. Pleasant skiing or snowshoeing is also possible up the North Fork of the Skokomish River.

The trail to Flapjack Lakes is the only good route into the touring area. From the lakes, it is another 1.5 miles to Gladys Divide. The best skiing is found in meadows near the divide, especially in the upper Hamma Hamma drainage, where a 2000-ft. run is available for the hardy.

Required map is the 15-minute Mt. Steel USGS quadrangle.

ENCHANTED VALLEY-QUINAULT RIVER

This area is recommended as a spring oversnow trip to view avalanches and spectacular waterfalls off the cliffs of Chimney Peak and vicinity. The trail distance is 11 miles to the Enchanted Valley Chalet, a large public shelter. A minimum of 2 days is recommended for this trip.

The tour starts at the end of the Quinault River road (see Climbing Routes, page 148, for approach details) and follows the river in timber most of the way to the chalet. The river crossing just below the chalet may be a problem. The open meadows above the chalet provide an excellent viewpoint; however, remember that these meadows were formed by avalanche. This trip is best in early spring, when conditions are more stable in the valley, and the road is passable to the trail.

Required maps are the 15-minute Mt. Christie and Mt. Steel USGS quadrangles.

MOUNTAIN SAFETY

In mountaineering our aim is to make sure of the highest form of
adventure consistent with our sense of proportion.
—GEOFFREY WINTHROP YOUNG

This guidebook has been compiled with the assumption that the
user is not a climbing novice—that he has acquired at least a
minimum level of skill on rock and snow, in routefinding and
wilderness navigation, and in survival, first aid, and dealing with
emergencies. Nevertheless, Olympic Mountain Rescue feels that
some basics need to be stressed repeatedly; also, that in certain
respects the Olympic Mountains differ from other nearby ranges.
The climber needs to adjust his preparation and techniques to
cope with these differences. The following information on accident prevention, survival, first aid, self-rescue, and rescue, is
keyed to the Olympics in an effort to meet these needs.

ACCIDENT PREVENTION

Climbing mountains is an exciting and satisfying form of recreation for an ever-increasing number of people. Unfortunately, the
probability of accidents becomes greater as the number of participants increases. However, nearly all accidents can be pre-
vented. The prudent mountaineer by preparing himself mentally,
physically, and with thorough training, learns to recognize
potentially dangerous situations before an accident occurs. If an
accident does happen, he is able to cope with it efficiently.

Unlike most forms of recreation, mountaineering is usually prac-
ticed in remote areas, perhaps days from ready communication,
transportation, outside help, and medical care. Therefore, the
importance of developing mountaineering skills, safe climbing
attitudes, and good physical condition cannot be overstressed.

Inner Constance, Mt. Constance, and Lake Constance (Dave Sicks)

Just one person in poor physical condition can endanger an entire party of climbers.

Weather is an extremely important factor in mountaineering. The Olympics generally enjoy a moderate climate, but it is not uncommon to experience a range of temperatures from subfreezing to 90°, and to see rain, snow, hail, and wind, as well as sunshine, within the space of a few hours. Regardless of the season, clothing for all conditions should be worn or carried, including a windproof parka; a woolen shirt or sweater; woolen trousers, socks, and mittens; sturdy, waterproofed boots with lug soles; and a rain coat or poncho. Adequate clothing not only serves to comfort the climber, but adds a large measure of safety. A weatherproof tarp or tent and a good sleeping bag are necessities in the Olympics. A knowledge of emergency shelters such as brush lean-tos and snow caves is invaluable in case of a forced bivouac.

Skill in the use of map, compass, and altimeter is especially vital in wilderness areas of the Olympics. Finding the way off a fogged-in mountain top or out of a brush-filled valley bottom may depend entirely on a knowledge of these navigational tools.

Personal first aid supplies should be included in each climber's pack, and a more comprehensive set of supplies should be added for the party venturing into a remote area for an extended period of time. The most vital assistance provided during an emergency will be rendered by the climbing party itself.

Avalanches are most frequent in this range during winter and spring. However, a snow slope can avalanche anytime during the year, given the right set of conditions. The experienced climber learns to recognize conditions which create avalanches, and avoids potentially dangerous terrain. Be especially wary of climbing up under snow cornices or beneath rock cliffs topped with heavy winter or spring snow. These masses of snow are certain to fall—don't be a target! Avoid steep, convex slopes, if possible, as they tend to fracture and avalanche when disturbed. Climbing straight up or down these slopes is always preferable to traversing them. If a steep slope must be crossed, it should be done at the top, where an avalanche is less likely to be triggered.

An ice axe should be carried at all times in the Olympics. Snow may be encountered throughout the summer, especially on northern exposures and in gullies, as the range abounds in permanent snowfields and small glaciers. Climbers should be thoroughly competent in self-arrest on all types of snow. A thorough knowledge of ice axe belays is a necessity, as is skill in glissading on all types of snow. Travel on living glaciers will be necessary on some of the major peaks. Never cross a glacier unless roped. Two rope teams are recommended as a minimum. A party traveling on glaciers must possess a thorough knowledge of crevasse-rescue techniques.

The traveler off the trails in the Olympics will encounter more than his share of loose or friable rock. This condition is further complicated by the presence of wet moss or lichen, especially in the transition zone between forest and peak. The combination makes much of the climbing more than normally hazardous. A hard hat with a secure chin strap is strongly recommended. Take care to stay out of the fall line of climbers above, and keep parties bunched closely when climbing in gullies.

Most of the rock climbing areas of the range are composed of metamorphic rock commonly called "pillow lava." This rock, while usually solid, has several characteristics which can trap the unwary. Holds are usually large (basketball size), rounded, and sloping. As such, they do not provide the security offered by angularly-cleft granite. In addition, the rock structure provides few good belay points. Climbers thus tend to overextend leads, which increases the risk of serious accidents. Therefore, it is recommended that iron be placed sooner than in most other ranges in the United States. "Pillow lava" is noted for a lack of piton cracks, and those present are often shallow or otherwise inadequate. When choosing an assortment of pitons for climbing in this range, include a good variety of angles and knifeblades. The paucity of cracks makes it advisable to take a bolt kit on all serious rock climbs.

Early starts are advisable, for the approaches are often exceptionally long and the elevation gain may be great. It is wise to bivouac when off trail, rather than attempt travel by night. Olympic river and stream crossings are usually hazardous, especially in the afternoon when swollen with melt-water. The prevalence of canyons, waterfalls, and insecure snow bridges in the high country adds to the potential danger.

Mountain Goats at Lake Constance (George W. Martin)

Though the Olympics differ from other ranges at least in degree, in many of the aforementioned factors, the skills necessary for safe climbing are basically the same. The experienced and considerate mountaineer will adjust to differing situations and will take into account the strengths and weaknesses of others in his party. He has the ability, tempered with caution, to reduce the probability of accident to an absolute minimum. The best way to prevent accidents and emergencies is to carry the "Ten Essentials" and to follow the condensed "Climbing Code" developed by generations of experienced mountaineers.

TEN ESSENTIALS	CLIMBING CODE
Extra food	Minimum of three—two rope teams on a glacier
Extra clothing	Carry necessary food, clothing, and equipment
Candle	Rope up on all exposed places and glaciers
Compass	
First aid kit	Keep party together, obey leader or majority rule
Flashlight	Never climb beyond your ability
Sun glasses and cream	Judgment must not be swayed by desire when choosing route or turning back
Knife	Leave trip schedule with a responsible person
Map	Follow the precepts of sound mountaineering
Matches	Deport yourself in a manner that will reflect favorably on mountaineering

SURVIVAL

The Olympic Peninsula provides some special problems and opportunities for survival. The following paragraphs emphasize some of these for the visitor to the area.

If You Are Lost

The basic rules apply here, as in other wilderness terrain. First, stop! Whistle or shout to attract the attention of other members of your party. Since panic is your greatest enemy, try to remain calm. Conserve your energy. Carefully review the situation so that you can formulate a plan to solve the problem. After retracing your recent movements in your mind and marking your present location, backtrack to the point where the route is again familiar.

If this fails, give some thought to establishing a camp where you can survive and attract the attention of searchers. Ideally, such a camp should provide an adequate wood and water supply, and natural shelter or the potential for building a makeshift shelter. It should be along the edge of open country where the smudge of a green bough fire will be visible and not be dissipated in the towering trees, and where searching aircraft can be signaled. Make camp at least 2 hours before sunset and gather plenty of firewood to last through the night.

The scarcity of dry tinder in the damp Olympic Range makes fire-building an exasperating chore in wet weather unless one carries candles or fire starters in his emergency pack. Watch for flakes of pitchy wood on the sides of rotten stumps and dead snags. These will burn even when soaking wet.

If the weather is favorable, a side-trip to the most convenient observation point may enable you to locate familiar landmarks. Give the international distress signal (three of anything, audible or visible) frequently throughout the first 2 days and evenings. Inventory your equipment, food, and other resources. Conserve your strength—important either for finding your own way out or for walking out when you have been located by a search party. Ration your food and matches as necessary. If after 2 days it seems apparent that you will not be found by searchers, it is time to consider walking out. When you break camp, be sure to leave a note or sign indicating the time, date, and your direction of travel. When you reach civilization, notify the nearest ranger station so that any search effort in progress can be terminated.

Travel

The Olympic Peninsula, like other wet coastal areas, has heavy undergrowth which makes cross-country travel both slow and difficult. Ridges are generally drier and more open, affording less hazardous and arduous travel than following streambeds, as is generally recommended elsewhere. Many main drainages in the Olympics have well-maintained trails adjacent to the streams, but there are enough exceptions to make a choice of stream travel questionable. Some major drainages, such as the Goldie, Queets, Tunnel Creek, and Silt Creek are notorious for their box canyons and frequent waterfalls in deep gorges. Many streams have a steep loss of elevation in their upper reaches, with areas of smooth, mossy rock and frequent cliffy falls which provide great hazard and result in slow and exhausting travel. When the drainage does bench out, one may have to contend with the notorious "green jungle," a prolific growth of slide alder, vine maple, willow, and devil's club. In selecting a drainage to follow, it may not be possible to determine whether it will lead to the Pacific Ocean, the Strait of Juan de Fuca, or Hood Canal, due to the radial drainage pattern of the range. Many streams and some major rivers flow into uninhabited areas where there is little chance of obtaining help or of being seen until one reaches the Olympic Highway.

In most cases, it is advisable to stay high and follow broad ridges or the alpland near timberline, downstream, paralleling a major drainage. This allows you to continue to search for familiar landmarks or fire lookouts, and you may see roads, trails, or logging activity in the adjacent valleys. You will also be in a position to signal searching aircraft with a mirror or bright clothing or tarp. If the ridge that you have chosen terminates at the confluence of two streams, forcing you to the river bottom, check both sides of the river for trails or roads before continuing.

Most large streams are too deep, fast, cold, and slippery to be crossed in any season without the aid of a rope. However, streams which are raging torrents in the afternoon may be fordable in early morning.

The generalization that moss grows on the north side of trees does not apply in this fog-shrouded range. It may grow on all sides, varying only with the prevailing local surface winds.

Native Foods

The Olympics provide many edible plants—starches, fruits in season, greens for teas, and other foods. Some are tasty, and some are merely good for you.

Most of the starchy foods come from the roots and bulbs of plants, and can be eaten raw by peeling off the outside skin, although they will usually be more palatable if boiled or roasted. Examples include blue camas root, cattail, deer fern, bracken, horsetail, yellow pond-lily, thistle, wapato or arrowhead, and wild onion.

Few of our fruits, berries, and seeds will make a person sick, and all have food value and flavor. Strawberry, blackcap, blackberry, salmonberry, thimble berry, red and blue huckleberry, wild cherry and plum, chokecherry, and black elderberry are among the more common varieties of fruits. The red elderberry has an unpleasant taste but is harmless. The berry of the Oregon grape is good for alleviating thirst. The meat from rose hips makes good food, as does salal berry, hazlenut, and the pine nut (located at the base of each flake in a pine cone).

There are also innumerable above-ground plants that can be used as greens, brewed for tea, or eaten raw as salads. These have more limited food value. They include both red and white clover (leaves, blossoms, and stems), dandelion (new leaves), fireweed, water cress, and wood sorrel. The white avalanche lily and its less common cousin, the yellow glacier lily, are especially desirable because all parts have food value. The white inner bark and tender buds of evergreen trees can also be used for food. The inner bark of aspen and alder are especially sweet, but care should be taken not to confuse alder with cascara. The dark green leaf of cascara is rough textured, and the veins curve parallel with the serrated edges to the apex. Avoid eating any part of cascara.

Many kinds of fungi and lichens have food value. Among these are the cream-colored mosses that grow on the ends of downed logs, the green hairy mosses hanging from trees, and the green mosses resembling seaweed that grow on dead wood. These, however, require careful and prolonged preparation. First soak for several hours, then dry and pound before cooking, and finally boil for about 20 minutes. Fresh puff balls can be fried or eaten raw. Mushrooms should be utilized *only* if the user is thoroughly familiar with identification of the various toxic and non-toxic varieties. In the spring, yellow pollen from trees collects on the surface of slow-moving streams and at the ends of wind-drifted lakes. This is high in food value, and can be collected and eaten.

Many small animals can be used for emergency food. However, these defenseless creatures should not be taken except in extreme situations. If the need for food is paramount, the porcupine, squirrel, rabbit, beaver, muskrat, marmot, and various other rodents are the best bet. While many of these are difficult to catch, some are curious and can be snared or clubbed as they emerge from their burrows. The porcupine is especially vulnerable. Birds' eggs can be collected in season, and the blue grouse and ptarmigan can occasionally be caught in alpland with the bare hands. Fish and frogs are relatively easy to obtain, and should not be overlooked. A bounteous variety of foods are available on the saltwater beaches, including crabs, oysters, clams, sea cucumbers, snails, octopus, seaweed, and sea urchin eggs. Slit the underside of starfish to obtain eggs.

The following references give information on survival and edible plants:

Mountaineering: The Freedom of the Hills, published by The Mountaineers

Wild, Edible and Poisonous Plants of Alaska, Extension Bulletin F-40 of the University of Alaska Cooperative Extension Service

Food in the Wilderness, by Martin and Scott

50 Edible Plants of British Columbia, Handbook No. 1 of the B.C. Provincial Museum

Handbook and *Fieldbook* published by the Boy Scouts of America

101 Wildflowers of Olympic National Park, published by the University of Washington Press

Field Guide to Rocky Mountain Wildflowers, by Craighead, Craighead and Davis

SELF-PROTECTION

The hiker should be able to recognize and avoid such plants as poison oak (even its smoke can be toxic), nettles, and devil's club. If inadvertently contaminated, wash with soap and hot water as soon as possible. Rub infected areas with a 10% solution of tannic acid or strong tea. Plants to avoid eating include false hellebore, water hemlock, buttercup, wild sweetpea, vetches, and lupines. These latter sometimes absorb from the soil toxic amounts of minerals and alkaloids that can produce disagreeable effects.

There are no poisonous snakes or reptiles on the Olympic Peninsula, but mosquitoes and biting flies can be a bother. Bees, wasps, and yellowjackets are sometimes a problem in late summer and fall. Ticks are found in the dry rain shadow in the eastern segment of the range, and the body should be inspected for them after a hike through brushy areas. Ticks can sometimes be coaxed out by an application of kerosene or the heat and smoke of a glowing coal. Do not crush an imbedded tick, for its body fluids then contaminate the wound. After removal, wash thoroughly with soap and water. Clothing should be removed and hung at night, for ticks will climb to the top and they can be removed the next morning. The traveler must protect his food and equipment from the black bear, marmot, raccoon, skunk, and raven. Many frequently-used campsites have wire stretched between trees to provide a place to hang food out of reach of animals.

Electrical storms are not as common in this range as in other ranges in the nation, but are an occasional hazard. If caught in a lightning storm, stay away from lone trees, high points on ridges, and metal objects such as ice axes. Sit on a dry coiled rope, and *not* next to or tied into a stretched out climbing rope which will act as a conductor if wet.

Hypothermia, or the loss of heat from the body core (commonly called exposure), can be serious for the unprepared visitor to the mountains. Extra energy can be a demand in this range due to the rugged terrain and rapidly-changing weather conditions. The best prevention of hypothermia is provided by adequate food and clothing, and the avoidance of exhaustion. Stay as dry as possible and take shelter on the lee side of rocks, or seek other protection. The inclusion of a storm kit in your pack, with waterproof matches, fire starters, food, and a plastic shelter may save your life. Such a kit can be expanded into a full-scale survival kit by adding a whistle, signal mirror, some simple fishing gear, snare equipment, and a repair kit. This, together with the "Ten Essentials," will be adequate for most emergencies not involving injury.

To summarize, survival in emergencies is dependent on good physical condition, adequate equipment, the conservation and replacement of body heat and energy, and—most important of all—your knowledge combined with common sense, and a calm analysis of the problem.

IF AN ACCIDENT OCCURS

The enjoyment and challenge of a good climb changes to an unpleasant, dangerous situation in case of an accident. A small amount of preparation at home can equip a party of four or more to give reasonable treatment to the injured members and enable the party to be evacuated safely. If an accident occurs, take the following steps:

1. Immediately determine if the victim must be or can be moved before treatment. Move if necessary. *Factors to consider:* Danger of further fall, rockfall danger, weather condition, technical climbing problems, spine or neck injury, bleeding, or difficulty with breathing.

2. Evaluate party capabilities and environmental conditions. *Capabilities:* Party size, first aid and rescue skills, supplies and equipment, fuel, food, shelter. *Environment:*

Steepness and type of terrain, weather (precipitation, temperature, wind), distance above timberline and from road end and help.

3. If party size and ability will permit self-rescue, do so. If the party will be delayed beyond the expected return time, send out two people with *written* information to be phoned to family to prevent undue anxiety. If help is needed, send two people with a *written* description of the accident including:

    1. Name, address, and age of persons involved.

    2. Location and terrain at accident scene and/or present location of party.

    3. Extent of known injuries; number of people involved; size, condition and ability of the remainder of the party; party equipment; weather at the scene.

The message for help should either be delivered in person or telephoned to the proper responsible agency. These are:

1. County Sheriff
2. Olympic National Forest District Ranger or Olympic National Park headquarters
3. The Mountain Rescue Council
4. The Washington State Patrol

If the phone number of the agency needed is not immediately available, contact the operator and secure her help in contacting one of the above agencies. The messengers should remain at a rendezvous point agreed on with the agency, for further interrogation or to guide the rescue party to the trailhead or accident site.

The person or persons remaining with the victim (the victim should *not* be left alone) will render first aid and make the entire party as comfortable as possible during the waiting period. Food, fuel, and shelter should be considered as soon as the immediate first aid is rendered. Build a fire in a protected place. During the waiting period, the most important thing is to keep the victim as comfortable as possible and in good spirits. Extra time can be spent in preparing meals and an especially comfortable shelter, thus improving the spirit of the entire party.

First Aid

The following comments are not meant to teach first aid for mountain travel, but to serve as a refresher on important points to be checked and treated. A standard first aid course should be mandatory and the advanced course is most desirable for anyone indulging in extensive back-country travel. Additional training can be gained by joining a ski patrol or mountain rescue unit.

Mountain Medicine by Fred T. Darvill, Jr., M.D. (published by the Skagit Valley Mountain Rescue Unit) is a useful pocket first aid text designed to be carried in the hills. A more comprehensive volume for home study and expeditionary use is *Medicine for Mountaineering,* edited by James A. Wilkerson, M.D. (published by The Mountaineers).

First aid in mountainous country follows the same rules as elsewhere. First establish an open airway: check for anything in the mouth or throat. Treat severe bleeding next, with pressure over the bleeding point. Beyond these immediate dangers, and the need to check for neck or spine injuries before attempting to move the victim, first aid treatment should be undertaken at a slower pace. This will tend to relax both the victim and the first-aider. Panic is apt to be present and must be controlled.

"Splint 'em where they lie" still fits. Traction should not be used under mountain conditions due to circulation and infection problems. Use fixation splints only. Apply direct pressure to control bleeding. Mouth-to-mouth artificial respiration can be used wherever the victim is, once the chest area is free of external pressure from snow, rock, or other debris. Note that such pressure could have caused cracked or broken ribs. Do not bind the chest for damaged ribs, as this restricts breathing and may lead to complications. If the victim is otherwise able to walk out, the chest may be bound to relieve pain, but only for the duration of the hike. Do not bind if there are broken rib ends which might be forced inward. A puncture through both skin and lung should be sealed immediately with any available wind-proof material, such as a plastic bag or a wet cloth. This patch should be sterile, but the patch itself is urgent.

Once the immediate injuries have been cared for, or even during this treatment, preventative measures for traumatic shock should be taken. Remove *all* damp or wet clothing. Reclothe the victim with sufficient insulation such as sleeping bags, parkas, etc., to retain normal body temperature. Provide shelter against rain, snow, and wind. Give liquid sparingly, and only to conscious victims with no abdominal injuries. Avoid causing vomiting if at all possible.

Accidental hypothermia, the loss of body heat faster than it can be replenished, can occur either in conjunction with traumatic shock or from a combination of fatigue and weather conditions. While not previously considered a first aid problem, hypothermia has been the cause of numerous deaths in the Olympics and Cascades. The surest treatment is prevention: good physical condition plus supplying the body's need for food and rest at regular intervals. Proper caloric intake, protection against wet and cold, and a positive mental attitude are the things to remember. Prevention is vital because the inability to think clearly occurs as a symptom. Once the brain is affected, the victim tends to ignore exhaustion, and death can be very rapid, sometimes within an hour.

Treat hypothermia immediately! Stop in a sheltered spot and get the victim into warm, dry clothing. Provide hot food, if possible, and hot drinks. A drink of hot jello will not usually upset even a nauseated person, and will supply quick energy. If the victim does not respond quickly and dramatically, or if he is extremely cold when discovered, apply external heat. This can be accomplished with a fire, stoves or lanterns in a shelter or tent, or direct body contact. If necessary, have an uninjured person strip and climb into a sleeping bag with the victim to warm him.

There is no reason for the prevalence of hypothermia if outdoor groups and climbing parties will observe a few simple recommended principles. These are:

1. Dress by the layer system, with wool next to the skin in cool weather, and windproof and waterproof outer garments. Keep the head and extremities warm.
2. Provide food and rest stops at regular intervals.
3. Establish a "buddy system" of observation by party members.

These few simple precautions will eliminate the headline, "Hiker Dies of Exposure."

NOTE: The following chart is intended only as a refresher under stress conditions for people with Red Cross or equivalent first aid training.

FIRST AID—GENERAL TREATMENT

INJURY	SYMPTOMS	TREATMENT
Severe bleeding	Blood pumping or spurting	Direct pressure. If cut at fracture, apply tourniquet 1 to 2 inches above wound. Use if bleeding restarts.
Suffocation	No sign of breathing	Open airway to mouth and throat. Mouth to mouth artificial respiration.
Broken neck	Pain in neck. Tingling or loss of sensation or inability to move limbs.	Immobilize upper body and head. Do not move victim without aid. Move as a log with direct upward pull on head and neck only when necessary.
Back injury	Pain in back. Tingling or loss of sensation or inability to move limbs.	Immobilize trunk and head in line. Do not move victim without aid.
Bone fracture	Visible deformity. Pain at injury, swelling, discoloration. Pain at injury caused by tapping adjacent joint with hand.	Splint, immobilizing adjacent joints. Check extremities for circulation. Protect extremities from cold. Knee should be splinted slightly bent if possible.

FIRST AID—GENERAL TREATMENT (*Cont.*)

INJURY	SYMPTOMS	TREATMENT
Traumatic shock	Skin pale, cool, then moist. Later, pulse rapid and weak, eyes dull, disoriented.	Victim prone on back. Head lowered unless head injury suspected. If conscious give tepid liquid unless abdominal injury suspected. Avoid causing vomiting if possible. Retain body heat by providing dry clothing and complete insulation from cold.
Frostbite (superficial)	No sensation in area, feels doughy. Color white, does not turn red after pressing.	Warm by warming the extremity against companion's armpit or abdomen.
Frostbite (severe)	No feeling in part. Color white. Part feels hard throughout.	Evacuate to location for sterile, rapid rewarming. Walk out on frozen injury if necessary. Stop when foot starts to thaw. Thaw in 104° water (warm to normal hand). Keep injury sterile once thawed. Do *NOT* use extreme heat (fire). Do *NOT* rub with snow or treat injury roughly. Do *NOT* thaw if re-freezing might occur.
Head injury	Period of unconsciousness. Check for fluid or bleeding from ears, nose, or mouth. Unequal pupil size. Loss of muscle power in any area. Disoriented.	Question victim to test judgment. When treating for shock, do not elevate feet. If symptoms are present, victim should be carried to aid as soon as possible. If no symptoms, observe patient's balance and walk him out with two or more companions as observers.
Fractured rib	Sharp pain when pressed. Breathing painful. Broken end may be depressed.	Sitting best position. Do *NOT* bind chest unless necessary to relieve pain for victim to walk out.

FIRST AID—GENERAL TREATMENT (*Cont.*)

INJURY	SYMPTOMS	TREATMENT
Hypo-thermia (expo-sure) (exces-sive loss of body heat)	Exhaustion, same symptoms as shock. Not mentally alert. Cold, but not thinking to warm self. Change in personality, usually disagreeable.	Food and rest in warm, shel-tered spot. Warm, dry clothing from skin out. Return body heat to normal by internal and external heat. Hot food and drink (when conscious). Heat near fire, stove, lantern in tent or shelter to raise air tempera-ture. Contact heat from a warm companion's body. Hot water bottle (canteen). Treat for shock.

SELF-RESCUE

Self-rescue without outside help is a formidable undertaking. However, the organization and implementation of a formal res-cue is no simple matter, either. Larger parties should consider carefully the possibility of self-rescue, providing the party is in good condition and the terrain is not extreme. If self-rescue is attempted, runners should still be sent for help in case the effort proves beyond the ability of the party.

Many climbing parties will be forced into using some self-rescue if an accident occurs in a site of such hostile nature that the vic-tim must be moved to a safer and more comfortable location. A climber falling into a crevasse or bergschrund, for example, can-not be left there to face inevitable death from hypothermic ex-posure. Avalanche or rockfall hazard may also necessitate move-ment of the victim, as may the impending onset of a storm. Beyond this immediate need, a full scale carryout should be at-tempted only after a thorough analysis of all pertinent factors, including:

1. Can the victim walk or help himself? A carryout is be-yond the capability of small parties if the victim is un-able to help himself. If the probability of further serious injury is small, an aided walkout is encouraged.

2. What is the party size, strength, condition, and technical ability? Two stretcher teams (12 people) will be needed if the distance is more than one mile.
3. How long will it take for help to arrive? Distance to the road is a factor.
4. Will the victim sustain further injury by transport on makeshift equipment?
5. Will delay in getting medical attention seriously threaten his life?
6. Is the terrain such that a carryout will place the victim or the rest of the party in undue jeopardy?
7. What sort of weather is expected during the carryout? Don't overlook the possibility of a helicopter pickup.

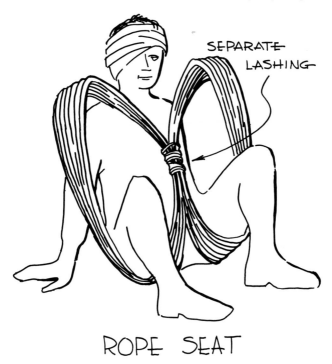

ROPE SEAT

Above all, think! If the decision is to evacuate, movement of the victim must be carefully planned and executed. In exposed areas, secure belays must be used to safeguard those involved in the transport as well as the victim. A handline, firmly anchored, is often a valuable asset. The small or inadequately equipped party can frequently protect their movements by the use of prusiks. The type of injury and the terrain will dictate the method of self-rescue. With a minor injury the victim may be able to descend fairly difficult pitches with only the help of a firm belay and an assisting companion. Keep in mind the danger of belated

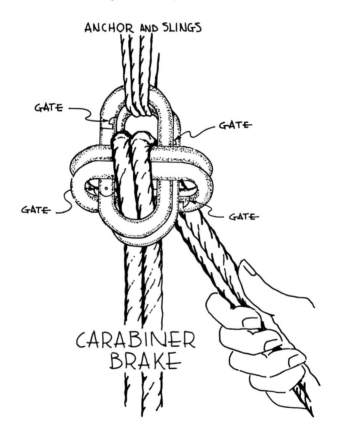

shock, mental or physical. More serious injuries will necessitate transport on some kind of makeshift stretcher or a simple rope seat used for a back carry.

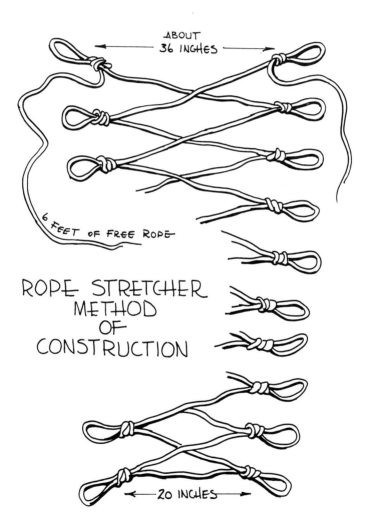

ABOUT 36 INCHES

6 FEET OF FREE ROPE

ROPE STRETCHER
METHOD
OF
CONSTRUCTION

20 INCHES

When the party arrives at timberline, a more comfortable stretcher from the standpoint of both the victim and carriers can be constructed from poles and parkas, ponchos, etc.

Lowering the injured party is best accomplished down the fall line. Since this is not always the route of ascent, scout ahead to avoid getting trapped. When lowering the stretcher, someone must be with the victim. This creates great tension on the rope, and calls for a carabiner brake system with sufficient friction to control the descent.

Ascent of a pitch or retrieval from a crevasse, which requires prusiking, bilgeri ascent, pulley systems, or cable systems, are beyond the scope of this book. For these techniques, climbers should study *Freedom of the Hills* by The Mountaineers, and *Mountain Rescue Techniques* by Wastl Mariner.

Accidents tend to occur when the hour is late and the party is tired, or when panic takes a hand. Self-rescue parties should plan each move with care. Decisions must be tempered with good judgment. The need for haste is frequently exaggerated, and serious mistakes are the result. During transport, the victim's welfare is paramount. Move him gently. Maintain his warmth. Check the circulation in his extremities often.

ORGANIZED RESCUE

When waiting for a rescue party, do not become impatient when help does not arrive immediately. The messengers, though traveling light, will usually take many hours to reach a telephone. After a responsibile agency such as the National Park Service is reached, the call for help will usually be relayed to a Mountain Rescue Unit. The organization of the rescue party is time-consuming; and though members can leave on short notice, long hours to the trailhead will use up additional time. Rescue teams travel on trails at night, but usually wait for first light before venturing into wilderness or technical terrain. A small, fast, advance party will usually arrive first to provide first aid and organize the details of a carryout or helicopter evacuation.

Those waiting with the victim should use this available time to provide for the comfort and well-being of the victim, and to mark the way to their location from some familiar landmark. Build a fire for warmth and morale. Since carryouts are difficult for both victim and rescuers, a path or trail should be cleared if possible. This will speed the evacuation immensely.

HELICOPTER RESCUE

Many rescues today are accomplished with great efficiency by helicopters. Most current helicopter support in the Olympics is provided by the Coast Guard at Port Angeles. Though their primary area of operation is the ocean and seashore, they have also become highly skilled in evacuation from mountainous terrain.

Helicopter rescue efforts can be greatly facilitated by proper ground assistance. The pilot must have a clear area 100 ft. in diameter. The many high lakes in the Olympics provide ideal landing sites for the float-equipped craft used by the Coast Guard. While waiting for a helicopter liftoff, police the landing or hovering site thoroughly to remove everything which might endanger the craft. If brush is cut, be sure to remove it completely, or it may be sucked into the rotors. The pilot must know the surface wind direction. While a smoke bomb is ideal, a smudge fire or a marker can provide this information.

Since the range of a helicopter is limited (dependent on the fuel supply), be ready for the pick-up when the craft arrives. Do not allow hope to rise too high. The onset of darkness, poor visibility, or cross winds may delay or prevent the pick-up. Success may also be precluded by the terrain or other ground conditions if it has not been possible to transport the victim to a good natural helispot. The party must stay in readiness for liftoff at a moment's notice, for changing weather conditions frequently allow only brief and intermittent air activity.

It is common practice for the Coast Guard to send a reconnaissance plane out first to locate the party. Since it is extremely difficult for people to be seen from the air, the presence of smoke, a message stamped in the snow, or bright cloth used as signal panels may determine whether the victim is evacuated one day or the next.

When preparing the victim for helicopter liftoff, and especially when the craft must hover over the area, extreme care should be taken to secure all loose material to prevent its entanglement in the rotors. Never use a tag-line from the ground to a hoisted party. Always approach a landed helicopter from the front, where you can be clearly seen by the pilot.

In summary, the chief factor leading to disaster is panic. Don't let this happen to your party. An accident is always serious, yet even the most adverse difficulties can frequently be overcome as long as good judgment and common sense prevail.

Mt. Cruiser (Dave Sicks)

Olympic Peaks 7,000 Feet or Higher

Mt. Olympus, West Peak	7,965
Mt. Olympus, Middle Peak	7,930
Mt. Deception	7,788
Mt. Olympus, East Peak	7,780
Mt. Constance	7,743
Inner Constance	7,670
Mt. Johnson	7,650
Mt. Mystery	7,631
Mt. Constance, South Summit	7,600
Sweat Spire	7,580
Martin Peak	7,550
Gasp Pinnacle	7,540
Mt. Clark	7,528
Gilhooley Tower	7,400
Mt. Walkinshaw	7,378
West Peak (Mt. Anderson Massif)	7,365
Athena	7,350
The Incisor	7,350
Mt. Anderson	7,321
Adelaide Peak	7,300
Warrior Peak, Southeast Summit	7,300
Warrior Peak, Northwest Summit	7,285
Gray Wolf Ridge	7,218
Cameron Peak	7,192
Mt. Mathias	7,168
Desperation Peak	7,150
Sundial	7,150
Mt. Fricaba	7,134
Echo Rock	7,100
Mt. Tom	7,048
The Arrowhead	7,000
Athena's Owl	7,000
Cloudy Peak	7,000
Curiosity Peak	7,000
Snifter Spire	7,000

PEAK INDEX

OTHER BOOKS FROM THE MOUNTAINEERS